Better Homes and Gardens®

Kitchens

YOUR GUIDE TO PLANNING AND REMODELING

BETTER HOMES AND GARDENS® BOOKS
Des Moines, Iowa

BETTER HOMES AND GARDENS® BOOKS
An Imprint of Meredith® Books

Kitchens: Your Guide to Planning and Remodeling
Writer/Editor: Linda Mason Hunter
Editor: Benjamin W. Allen
Associate Art Director: Lynda Haupert
Copy Chief: Angela K. Renkoski
Electronic Production Coordinator: Paula Forest
Production Manager: Douglas Johnston

Editor-in-Chief: James D. Blume
Director, New Product Development: Ray Wolf
Managing Editor: Christopher Cavanaugh
Vice President, General Manager: Jamie L. Martin

Meredith Publishing Group
President, Publishing Group: Christopher Little
Vice President and Publishing Director: John P. Loughlin

Meredith Corporation
Chairman of the Board and Chief Executive Officer: Jack D. Rehm
President and Chief Operating Officer: William T. Kerr
Chairman of the Executive Committee: E. T. Meredith III

Cover photograph: This open-plan kitchen is shown on page 8.

All of us at Better Homes and Gardens® Books are dedicated to providing you with information and ideas you need to enhance your home. We welcome your comments and suggestions about this book on kitchens. Write to us at: Better Homes and Gardens® Books, Do-It-Yourself Editorial Department, LN-112, 1716 Locust St., Des Moines, IA 50309–3023.

Contents

▲ *Hardwood flooring, schoolhouse pendant lights, and old-fashioned divided-light windows lend a timeless air to this thoroughly modern family kitchen in a 1928 Tudor home.*

Introduction

The kitchen has changed. No longer just a place for making and dishing out meals, the kitchen is now a main gathering spot, a place for the kids' homework, or a home office for paying bills.

It's also the most complex room in a house, both in design and technology. To be successful, it must work efficiently. To be efficient, it must be custom-tailored to fit the needs of the people using it in the way they cook and in the way they live. When the kitchen works well, its design promotes cooking efficiency and produces a warm, comfortable space.

Getting your kitchen to fit just right, aesthetically as well as functionally, will probably entail some degree of renovation. Kitchens designed even 15 years ago were not equipped to handle the needs of the modern American family. Cooks today want features such as three ovens, two sinks, and a compact area for quick food preparation. Consequently, designers are planning kitchens around specialized work centers: efficient combinations of appliances, storage systems, and countertops to maximize the use of space. While remodeling your kitchen may seem an overwhelming task, remember that even modest efforts will help when creating a better kitchen. Julia Child—renowned cook, author, and teacher—advises, "As long as you have enough space and good light and loads of room to hang and put things—even the ceiling if necessary—you'll be fine."

Renovating your kitchen to meet your needs now and into the next century makes good economic sense. Professionally executed, it can significantly increase the value of your house. According to *Remodeling Magazine*, kitchen remodeling reaps the biggest payback, dollar for dollar, of any room remodeling in the house.

Rest assured that planning and designing your kitchen is a manageable process. There's lots of help to guide you through it. Decades of collective design experience have produced guidelines for proper placement and space allocation for all the "hard goods:" fixtures, appliances, cabinets, and counters. But guidelines alone do not a great kitchen make. That's where people come into the equation. Whether you live in a household of one, four, or more, individual and group needs and preferences figure strongly into a kitchen's ultimate design.

How to Use This Handbook

Better Homes and Gardens® Kitchens: Your Guide to Planning and Remodeling takes you through the intricate process of planning and designing a kitchen remodeling. After completing all the phases in this book, you'll end up with a detailed sketch and a final plan for building, down to every electrical outlet and phone jack.

Now you're ready to take the first step: Dreaming. Fortunately, it's relatively effortless. Start by perusing home magazines, visiting kitchen displays, clipping advertisements, and making notes about kitchens you visit. Not only will this stimulate thinking about design, it will teach you how to become a savvy product shopper.

Phase One: "What Kind of Kitchen?" introduces you to the basic functions and layout possibilities. A checklist helps you evaluate your current kitchen and assess your family needs.

Phase Two: "Work Centers and Spaces" details the three hardworking kitchen centers—food storage and preparation, cooking, and cleanup. You'll learn how to design an efficient and workable plan for each center and get a look at sample remodelings before you settle on a solution that works for you and your lifestyle.

Phase Three: "Special-Order Kitchens" showcases a gallery of kitchens, each with a theme and a plan detailing how it works.

Phase Four: "Remodeling Strategies" helps you develop a plan for your remodeling. You may be among the lucky few who simply need to put a new face on your cabinets without changing the layout. Or, you may be seeking a complete overhaul—new surfaces and appliances, plus more work space. This section helps you decide how extensive your remodeling should be and gives you tips on estimating costs and setting a budget.

Phase Five: "Selecting Materials" deals with the nitty-gritty of surfaces and materials—cabinets, countertops, floors, ceilings, walls, windows.

Phase Six: "Choosing Fixtures and Appliances" is all about the things wired, plumbed, and ducted in to make the room work as it should.

Phase Seven: "Developing Your Design" takes you from recording every important dimension to completing a working drawing and compiling a detailed materials list. At this point, you can show your sketch to a design professional (a kitchen designer, architect, or interior designer) if you don't feel absolutely comfortable with it. Someone who's designed many kitchens can quickly spot flaws or missed opportunities and fine-tune details. Such help is well worth the fee. You also can give your final sketch to your cabinetmaker because you're ready to enter the last phase: Building.

Throughout the book we use the following abbreviations in sample floor plans of kitchens.

O=Wall ovens	MW=Microwave oven
R=Refrigerator/Freezer	F=Freezer
DW=Dishwasher	C=Compactor
W=Washer	D=Dryer

What Kind Of Kitchen?

PHASE 1: The first phase in the planning process is to decide what kind of kitchen you want.

How do you combine style and efficiency to create a kitchen that's certain to fit your family's needs now and into the next century? Believe it or not, it's close to a scientific process with a few basic rules and lots of guidelines to bridge the gap from before to after.

Like any big project, building a new kitchen is really a collection of parts and phases about which you must make decisions and take actions. Take them one at a time and the monolith becomes much more manageable.

So where do you start with a kitchen design? The first decision is what type of kitchen you want. This depends on how you choose to use it, the way you cook and live, and how much money you want to spend. Just about all kitchens can be classified among five types: basic and functional, eat-in, open-plan, family-oriented, and creative. Chances are one of these will suit the way your family lives and will serve as a springboard for developing your design.

The type design you choose will determine the layout. The shape and size will have the biggest influence on your layout decision, but don't feel hemmed in by your present floor plan. Things can be changed, a little or a lot, to make way for the kitchen you really want.

▲ *This kitchen is a family gathering room, designed for several people to work in at once. An old table serves as an island. The legs are trimmed to make it low enough for kids to help with kitchen chores.*

Basic Kitchen

Basic in features, function, and style, this is a no-frills kitchen. Small to medium in size, it can have any sort of layout, but it is designed primarily for food preparation, cooking, and cleanup and rarely includes areas for dining, sitting, or laundry, though they may be nearby.

◄ *A large pass-through to the dining room opens up this galley kitchen, which is only 6 feet wide.*

A Kitchen for Every Household

Eat-In Kitchen

An informal eating area in the kitchen is a tremendously popular feature. It needn't be elaborate or take up a lot of space. The simplest is a snack bar, an extra-wide counter a few inches higher than most dining tables, where people pull up stools and eat at the counter. At the other end of the spectrum is the breakfast room or dining nook, a space open and adjacent to the kitchen proper but still separate from it. Eat-in areas can be developed from existing space or from a small addition, such as a bump-out—an extension to the side of a house.

◄ *Here, the L-shaped peninsula defines a compact work core where the refrigerator, cooktop, and sink are within easy reach. Three stools pull up to the snack bar to make room for quick and easy meals.*

Open-Plan Kitchen

This approach with few walls involves space that is visually connected to other rooms, such as the dining room or family room. The kitchen space is defined by counters, cabinet islands, or peninsulas rather than walls. Like eat-in areas, open plans are quite popular today. The kitchen seems larger than its actual dimensions because it's not closed in. If you entertain frequently and informally, consider this approach so you can work in the kitchen and chat with your guests.

◄ *Few walls separate rooms in this airy bungalow. Cabinetry is low-cost modular units the owners painted. They routed out panels on the upper cabinets and installed glass to showcase dishware and spices.*

Family Kitchen

This is a large, full-featured kitchen connected to adjoining living and dining spaces to create an all-purpose family compound. This type has evolved only in the last few years as people have demanded an informal living space where the family gathers to eat, watch TV, do homework, play games, plan meals, or other activities. It may include a fireplace, an audio/video entertainment center, toy storage, and low, kid-accessible snack storage. To give children even more independence, some family kitchens have small, under-counter refrigerators and microwave ovens.

▼ *In the floor plan and photographs, right, an L-shaped space with island keeps visitors out of the way.*
■ *Extra-wide aisles allow two cooks to work at the same time.*
■ *A sink in the island creates a spot to make salads.*
■ *A fireplace is the focal point.*

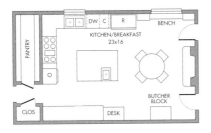

Creative Kitchen

This type could very well go by other names: gourmet kitchen, baker's delight, two-cook kitchen, super-kitchen. The point of this approach is that it goes all out to support a personal or family hobby, or that it simply overflows with features and functions—two sinks, two ovens plus a microwave, plenty of lighting, windows and skylights everywhere, maybe even a mini-greenhouse.

► *Created as a stage for a serious chef, this kitchen is actually a narrow galley plan. At one end, the cook has only to turn around from the small food-preparation sink to grab more fresh vegetables out of the refrigerator. The far end of the kitchen is a compact cleanup center.*

Rebuilding the Work Triangle

Efficiency in the kitchen used to be measured in steps; now it's measured in minutes. Mom grabs a muffin as she dashes out the door in the morning. Bobby races home from basketball practice and throws together a sandwich, munching it along the way to rehearsal for the school play. American kitchens have to be equipped to handle this fast-paced, everyone-for-themselves shuffle, as well as other modern needs, such as multiple cooks, kids, and crowds.

As a result, the 40-year-old commonsense concept of the work triangle (a path linking the three major kitchen components: refrigerator, sink, and cooktop) is undergoing revision. Even though the basic concept is still sound, designers are beginning to talk about designing a triangle within a triangle to handle both large and small meals. A secondary triangle, for example, might link a bar sink, the microwave, and refrigerator for frequent quick-fix meals. Some kitchen designers are advocating four separate work centers: a short-term food preparation area for quick meals, a long-term food preparation area, a cooking area, and a cleanup area.

In all fairness, the work triangle was a great concept when it was developed, but that was when the kitchen was a closed-in room with one cook. Now the walls are coming down. Modern kitchens are actually evolved keeping rooms that incorporate pass-throughs and an adjacent family room. Everybody's in the kitchen. The work triangle may not fit today's busy lifestyles exactly, but it at least gives you the ability to measure, in one simple method, the effectiveness of a kitchen layout (See the Basics of the Work Triangle, *below*). That is its strength.

Basics of the Work Triangle

The work triangle keeps the three primary work centers in close proximity, eliminating wasted effort and time. Measure the triangle from the center of the sink to the center of the refrigerator to the center of the cooktop. The perimeter of the triangle should measure no more than 26 feet and no less than 12 feet, according to the National Kitchen and Bath Association. No one side of the triangle should be greater than 9 feet or less than 4 feet. And the triangle should not be interrupted by traffic or cabinetry.

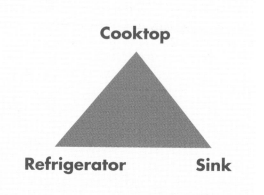

Shaping the Kitchen

Every kitchen has the same basic ingredients—cabinets, countertops, fixtures, appliances. It's how you arrange these givens that makes the difference, for better or worse, in the way your kitchen functions.

The layouts shown here cover the basic shapes of most kitchens and can be varied to work in your specific situation. Remember, you may be able to change the room if it doesn't let you have the kitchen you really want.

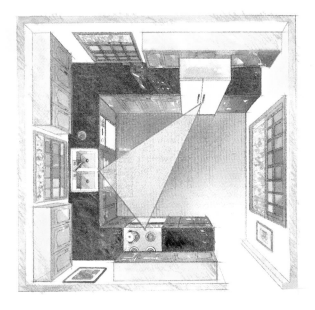

One-Wall

➤ *A close cousin to the galley is the single-wall kitchen, the least efficient layout. If that's the only arrangement available, locate the sink in the center with the range and refrigerator at opposite ends. If possible, include 4 feet of counter space on each side of the sink.*

U-Shaped

▲ *The most efficient and the most versatile kitchen layout. Having storage and counter space on three sides saves steps for the cook, and the dead-end design keeps the kitchen from becoming a household traffic artery. A U-shaped kitchen must be at least 8x8 feet to provide a minimum of 4 feet of working area in the center of the room. Conversely, a U-shaped kitchen that's too large may also cause problems by exceeding the maximum 26 feet for the work triangle.*

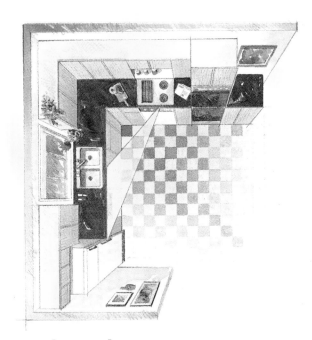

Galley

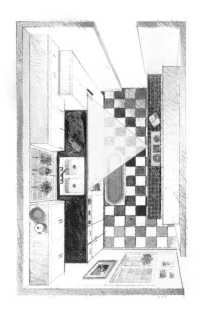

◄ *Parallel walls let the cook easily move from one work area to another. The drawback is that traffic is bound to flow through the work area unless one doorway is closed off. Place the refrigerator and sink on one wall and the range on the opposite one with 4 to 6 feet for the aisle.*

L-Shaped

▲ *The L-shaped kitchen requires less space than the U-shaped kitchen and can be almost as efficient. Two adjacent walls create a triangle that protects the cook from interference, especially if main work areas are kept close to the crook of the L. Work should flow from refrigerator to sink to cooking and serving areas. If you switch the order of the work centers, you could create more steps for yourself, making the plan less efficient.*

Consider an Island or Peninsula

Not only do islands and peninsulas increase efficiency they also let people prepare, cook, and clean up while looking out into the room, rather than against a wall. They are versatile, too. Use them for meal preparation, then clean them off to make a snack bar for informal eating. As a room divider, an island or peninsula becomes a buffet for setting out self-service meals during a party. They are popular sites for a cooktop and a second sink.

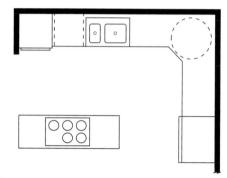

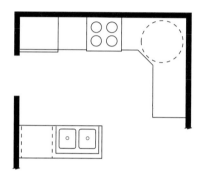

Plan on an Island

An island works well in U-shaped and L-shaped kitchens, shortening distance between work centers and directing traffic outside the main work core. In a U-shaped kitchen there should be more than 10 feet between legs of the U. Don't install an island in a kitchen where work areas are on opposite walls; you'll add needless extra steps. Leave at least 42 inches of walk space on all sides of the island; for two cooks, 48 inches is best.

Plan on a Peninsula

Unlike a freestanding island, one short end of a kitchen peninsula attaches at a right angle to a wall or a bank of cabinets. A peninsula is just as versatile as an island, but it doesn't require as much floor space. If you have floor space available in your kitchen but have run out of wall space, the peninsula may be the perfect solution.

DESIGN DETAIL

■ An island or peninsula designed with several workstations is ideal for two or more cooks. Try varying the heights of workstations to assure a comfortable spot for everyone.
■ Top the island or peninsula with a cooktop to handle cooking duties, include a small sink for washing vegetables, or just go for expanses of unbroken work surface.
■ Moving the sink to an island or peninsula is not that complicated or expensive if you have a basement with accessible plumbing.

■ In large kitchens, islands are an ideal location for task-specific countertops, such as butcher block for chopping vegetables or marble for rolling out pastry dough.
■ Don't forget to place an electrical outlet in the island for small appliances.
■ If you know you'll regularly be using countertop appliances on an island or peninsula— say for mixing or baking—plan storage space for them close at hand.

PLAN ON IT

KITCHEN
17x9

DW

BRKFST
14x10½

R

W   D

Before

KITCHEN
9x17

DW

BRKFST
9x16

C

DESK   R

D   W

After

▲ *The island in this galley kitchen stretches the work space separating the kitchen from the breakfast room without shutting them off from each other. To achieve a larger kitchen, the homeowner claimed an adjacent hallway. Then he combined the old kitchen and breakfast area into a family space including room for a table, desk, television, and door to the deck. At the hub of the plan is a versatile island that includes a second sink and a snack bar with stools along one side.*

Plan Adequate Storage

Ample and organized storage for food and utensils is the thread that holds an efficient kitchen together. Without it, working in the kitchen can be a never-ending hunt for the item you need.

As you plan additional storage, keep in mind that the location of this storage space is just as important as the amount. If your new storage is beyond reach, you'll just create new problems without solving old ones.

◄ *Instead of using a sliver of space for a broom closet that would hold little more than a broom, install a nifty pullout pantry like this one. Adjustable shelves hold everything from canned goods to boxes of breakfast cereal.*

► *A vintage surface treatment also serves as a disguise for shelf space for appliances and cabinetry. Here, sheets of embossed tin intended as ceiling panels cover the front of a pantry. The embossed metal mimics the punched-tin panels found on many antique cupboards and pie safes. Note the pantry stops short of the ceiling, an effective way to make built-in cabinetry look more like furniture.*

▲ *A pullout drawer keeps this toaster oven handy for use at breakfast. It's out of sight and out of the way when not in operation. An electrical outlet installed at the rear of the drawer ensures easy use.*

▼ *A cluster of canisters can cramp your work space, so store flour, sugar, and other ingredients in overhead cubby drawers.*

➤ *Appliance garages keep clutter to a minimum. Here, two tambours are closed; one is open to reveal a food processor ready for use.*

▲ *Half-circle lazy Susan shelves keep this corner cupboard from becoming a dead end. This is a good way to tackle dish storage if you have children in the house. They can help set the table, since dishes are stored within reach.*

▲ *This slick shelf puts the mixer at just the right height for an avid baker. When folded down, the shelf still allows plenty of room for the mixer in the cupboard. The sliding cover on the bread drawer makes a nice work surface for a helper.*

▲ *A sliding rack for pots and pans will make your life easier. Grab handles without having to bend over, and see at a glance which pot best fits your cooking plans. Use space in the bottom of the cabinet for baking sheets.*

Check Your Storage

✔ Store items as close as possible to the relevant appliance or the counter where you use them.

✔ As a general rule, store utensils and food staples according to how frequently you use them. Frequently used items go in front unless they are so large that they block access to items behind them.

✔ Store items by weight, with the heaviest ones placed between hip and shoulder height. Put the lightest items above your head.

✔ Duplicate frequently used utensils, such as paring knives, herbs, and spices, at different work centers.

✔ Plan specialized storage, such as cubbies, bookshelves, and appliances garages, at counter level.

Assess Your Needs

Good planning is the foundation of any remodeling. If you don't plan well, you can't expect to get the most cost-effective solution to your problem. Smart planning takes time. Don't rush the process. According to experts, you should spend as much time planning and designing the remodeling as it takes for actual construction.

Analyze How You Live

Before any tangible planning takes place, you need to analyze the way you cook. Good design rests on knowing how you like to cook. If you think about how you cook, you'll make better decisions on what gear you need and where it belongs in your kitchen.

How Do You Use the Kitchen?

❑ Do you prepare lots of elaborate meals, or are microwave dishes your forte?
❑ Do the kids help themselves after school?
❑ Is your kitchen often the site of specialized activities, such as grilling, baking, or canning?
❑ Do you do a lot of chopping?
❑ Do you insist on an uncluttered work area?
❑ Is continuous counter space important? For many cooks, this is the key to a good kitchen.
❑ Do you need to accommodate more than one cook at a time?

Once you decide if your kitchen is the domain of just one family cook or an arena of chefs, you'll have a better grasp of what to anticipate in arranging work centers, allocating space, and choosing the kind and number of appliances. You may also discover a need for spaces suited for bookkeeping, study, or play.

How Do You Entertain?

❑ How many guests and how often?
❑ Is your house the site of family holiday celebrations? How many does that entail?
❑ Do guests gravitate to the kitchen to socialize?
❑ Do your children bring friends home?

Maybe you'd like to include in your plan a serving buffet, a wet bar, or a center just for preparing snacks. Perhaps a large cleanup center is in order for taking care of dishes after elaborate holiday meals.

Review Long-Range Plans

❑ How do you expect your kitchen will be used in the next three, five, and ten years?
❑ What remodeling changes do you expect the house to accommodate?
❑ Will teenagers soon be out of the house?
❑ Do you often have weekend guests?

A large family's kitchen needs more of just about everything: more dining space, work centers, storage. If you're just starting a family, you'll want a plan suited to the safety and comfort of young children. If your kids are already teenagers, they may like to do some of the cooking. Also, look to the day when your kitchen will serve just the two of you or you alone.

Determine Limits

To what extent do you want to remodel? Here are the basic choices:
■ repair what's deteriorated or defective
■ enhance existing space by adding more light, getting new furniture, and/or decorating with paint or wall coverings
■ rearrange existing space by adding or removing walls, windows, and/or doors
■ convert unused space
■ build an addition

If you need more space, you may have to expand the parameters of your remodeling. Perhaps you can knock down a wall and borrow space from another room. Adding a 3-foot bump-out may give you all the space you need.

Take Inventory

Take a good, hard look at your kitchen. Analyze it from every angle using this inventory as a guide. Concentrate on arranging your cooking tools to suit your convenience.

❏ Is there a place to put down groceries when you come home from shopping?
❏ Is there counter space next to the sink for dirty dishes?
❏ Do you have difficulty storing things in corner cabinets?
❏ Can you store dishes near your dishwasher?
❏ Are pots and pans stored where you can get them easily?
❏ Is there a place to store potatoes and onions near the sink?
❏ You shouldn't have to make more than one step between the stove and the refrigerator and the sink and your cutting board.
❏ Is there wasted space on shelves because spice jars coexist with cereal boxes?
❏ Do you have good light over each counter surface so you can see what you are doing?
❏ Do you have one window that can be opened?
❏ Is the range vented to the outside?
❏ Do you have non-slip flooring?
❏ Is a fire extinguisher handy?

Things to Consider

Is the work flow uninterrupted? Traffic should flow around the kitchen's work triangle. If it doesn't, there are apt to be collisions between the cook and anyone passing through.

Do you have enough storage space where you need it? Basic storage standards suggest 18 square feet of cabinet space plus 6 additional square feet for each family member. Plan storage space near where the item will be used: pot storage near the range and food storage near the mixing center. You'll need space for cool storage: 12 cubic feet (refrigerator/freezer) for two people. Add 2 cubic feet for each additional person.

Is there optimum space between work centers? It's best to allow 4 to 9 feet between the range and refrigerator; 4 to 7 feet between the refrigerator and the sink; and 4 to 6 feet between the sink and the range. Tighten up this work triangle and you've created a traffic jam. Allow too much space and you'll need track shoes to work in your kitchen.

Is there counter space near each work center? Counter space on both sides of the sink (18 to 24 inches on each side) is a must. You also need space near the refrigerator (15 inches on the handle side) to set foods, a heat-resistant space near the microwave oven and wall ovens (15 to 18 inches on one side) to set hot pans, and room around the cooktop (12 to 18 inches on each side) for supplies.

Can you make room for eating? If you're short on space, consider a counter eating area that can double as food-preparation space. For a table and chairs, plan a minimum of 32 inches between the table and the wall.

What do you dislike most about your current kitchen?
❏ Lack of space
❏ Too little storage
❏ Poor lighting
❏ Layout, floor plan
❏ Outdated colors and decorating
❏ Worn out cabinetry, flooring, mechanical systems
❏ Outdated appliances
❏ Other

What features do you want most in your new kitchen?
❏ Recycling
❏ Continuous counter space
❏ An additional sink, oven, or dishwasher
❏ An island or peninsula
❏ An eating area
❏ A pantry
❏ Other

Work Centers And Spaces

PHASE 2: Determine the functions of your new kitchen to develop a design.

While using a work triangle solves many design problems, today's kitchen designs go much further. Now designs accommodate kitchens with three ovens or two sinks, kitchens without walls on all sides, and additional family activities like doing homework, eating, and entertaining.

Although the work triangle connecting the refrigerator, sink, and stove functions well for the single user, when it comes to a kitchen the whole family uses, it's time to start thinking in terms of work centers. There are basically three of these in every kitchen—food storage and preparation, cooking, and cleanup.

Try to provide 36 inches of counter for every person who uses the kitchen regularly. Organize 36-inch sections of counter according to the tasks that will be performed there, such as kneading, chopping, and stacking dirty dishes. These are the work centers. After you have defined them, apply the principles of the work triangle to make moving between them more efficient.

The Live-in Family Kitchen

Shown on page 20 are two versions of the live-in family kitchen—a maxi version that's 200 square feet and a mini version that's approximately 100 square feet. Both are open-ended making it easy to cook without interruptions from the multiple activities the rooms accommodate. Both involve an
continued

➤ *Green stained antique-looking cabinets set the tone in this old-house kitchen. The 8-foot-long island makes a great buffet for serving large numbers of people.*

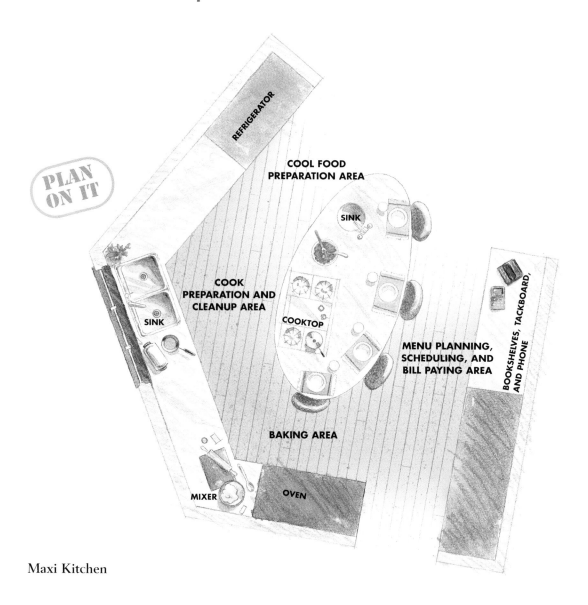

PLAN ON IT

REFRIGERATOR

COOL FOOD PREPARATION AREA

SINK

COOK PREPARATION AND CLEANUP AREA

SINK

COOKTOP

MENU PLANNING, SCHEDULING, AND BILL PAYING AREA

BOOKSHELVES, TACKBOARD, AND PHONE

BAKING AREA

MIXER

OVEN

Maxi Kitchen

island for diverse uses—a place for guests to hang out while food is being prepared; a buffet for snacks; a space to open mail, talk on the phone, or read the newspaper.

The maxi version uses a 60-degree angle rather than the standard 90-degree or 45-degree angle. Common in much of Frank Lloyd Wright's later work, the 60-degree angle works well in a live-in kitchen because it allows traffic to flow evenly in and around the room.

For those who don't want a major investment, the mini plan takes up only 100 square feet, works for two people, and includes many of the features of the larger plan, including a 50-inch-high counter, which gives the cooking side a low wall to hide kitchen equipment in an open plan.

REFRIGERATOR

50"-HIGH COUNTER

RANGE

COOL FOOD PREPARATION AREA

COOK PREPARATION AND CLEANUP AREA

SINK

DW

Mini Kitchen

Hardworking Centers

Food Storage and Preparation

Busy families now spend more time heating up takeout food or leftovers than preparing meals from scratch. New food storage and preparation workstations now include a snack center, which might have a small microwave oven, a wrapping station for lunches and leftovers, and even a second sink. It also can work for weeknight meals.

Still, this work center must be equipped to accommodate weekend cooks who enjoy making a big meal. Plan well-organized storage for canned and dry goods, mixing bowls, casserole dishes, cookbooks, and small appliances.

The best cabinets for food storage are those attached to cool outside walls, near shaded north-facing windows. Cabinets near heat sources—including the dishwasher, oven, refrigerator, and southern exterior walls—are not the best choices for storing foods. Consider putting one section of countertop a few inches lower than the rest so it's easier for kids to make their own snacks.

The latch side of the refrigerator should face into the work triangle and the door should open completely so bins can be pulled out with ease. The refrigerator door also should not swing into a doorway.

MEASUREMENTS

- Plan for 36 inches of uninterrupted counter space close to a water source.
- If cabinets stretch into a corner, install units along adjoining walls for a lazy Susan.
- Leave at least 15 inches of counter space next to the handle side of the refrigerator. Or, put a 15-inch space within 48 inches across from the refrigerator.
- To increase floor space, consider a refrigerator that is only 24 inches deep instead of the standard 30 or 33 inches.
- A refrigerator with a freezer on the top or bottom will take up a space 28 to 30 inches wide. Side-by-side models range from 30 to 36 inches wide.

Cooking

The main ingredients of the cooking center are the cooktop or range and the microwave oven. A conventional oven separate from the cooktop is likely to be your least-used appliance and, as such, can be placed outside the work triangle.

The cooking center requires ample storage for pots and pans, utensils, pot holders, hot pads, spices and seasonings, and food products that go directly from storage container to simmering pot.

The cooktop is most efficient and safest with at least 18 inches of counter space on each side. This enables you to turn handles away from traffic and set down hot pots. Use a heat-resistant countertop surface around the range.

Another component of the cooking center is a ventilation system (see pages 87 and 88). The system you choose should be directly vented outside and have a fan that blows a minimum of 150 cubic feet of air per minute.

MEASUREMENTS

■ Leave 15 to 18 inches of open counter space near the microwave oven for setting hot dishes.
■ Place your microwave oven so it's 2 inches below the primary user's elbow and 10 inches above it.
■ Wall oven height should leave the open door 5 to 7 inches below the cook's elbow.
■ Leave 18 to 24 inches of counter space on each side of the cooktop. If the cooktop is in an island, leave at least 12 inches on each side.

■ Leave 16 inches of clearance between the center of the front burner and a wall or cabinet. Leave 14 inches between the center of the front burner and a turn in the countertop.
■ Leave 27 to 36 inches of clearance between a range or cooktop and an overhead cabinet.
■ Don't put a cooking surface below an operable window unless the window is more than 3 inches behind the cooking unit and 24 inches above it.

Cleanup

The sink not only is the star of the cleanup center, it also plays a supporting role in the food preparation and cooking centers. Because of that, the sink should be placed at the center of the work triangle, between the range and refrigerator.

Other major components of the cleanup center are the garbage disposal and the dishwasher, so dirty plates can be scraped and loaded into the dishwasher without lost steps. The dishwasher should be placed to the left of the sink if you are right-handed, to the right if you are left-handed.

Storing everyday glasses, dishes, and utensils near the dishwasher is one option, but you may want to move some of those items to more convenient locations near the table or in the snack area of the food preparation center.

If you plan to use a trash compactor, have it installed on the side of the sink opposite the dishwasher. This saves steps and makes effective use of the countertop.

Plan storage space for dish towels, cleaning products, and a trash receptacle. The cleanup center is also an ideal spot for a recycling system.

MEASUREMENTS

■ Leave 36 inches of counter space on each side of the sink, if possible. If space is tight, retain a minimum of 24 inches on the dishwasher side and 18 inches on the other.

■ Keep 2 inches of space between the front edge of the sink and the edge of the counter.

■ Leave 22 inches of clearance between the sink rim and an overhead cabinet.

■ Place the center of the sink bowl at least 14 inches from a turn in the counter.

■ Allow 21 inches of standing room between the dishwasher and adjacent counters, other appliances, and cabinets.

■ The dishwasher should be within 36 inches of the sink for maximum efficiency.

■ Double sinks require a 36-inch base cabinet; single sinks need a 30-inch base cabinet.

■ If a second sink is part of the plan, at least 3 inches of counter space is needed on one side, 18 inches on the other.

Nice-to-Have Centers

▲ *This custom roll-top kitchen desk, located below a skylight, houses the family computer and a couple of file drawers.*

▼ *Recycling is a cinch with this partitioned drawer. Plastic bins separate plastic, glass, and tin. A canvas bag at the back collects newspapers.*

Planning

A planning center is a valuable addition to any kitchen. Though the nook, *left*, takes up 48 inches of wall space, as little as 30 inches is needed to create a spot for a telephone or a home computer, where you can organize recipes, have a home office, or have the kids study.

Isolate the desk at the end of the kitchen, but tie it in with the kitchen's design by using cabinets and drawers in the same style as the room's other cabinets.

The desk top should be 30 inches off the floor and the kneehole at least 24 inches wide. A pencil drawer adds convenience, and you can hang a bookshelf on the wall above the desk.

Also important are adequate lighting, an easy-maintenance desk surface, and a message center.

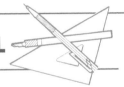

DESIGN DETAIL

■ Minimum desk top size is 24 inches wide and 20 inches deep.
■ Standard desk top height is 30 inches, about 6 inches lower than standard counter-top height.
■ Allow at least 30 inches of clearance for pulling out the desk chair.

Recycling

To organize recycling, install a drawer with room for three or four plastic containers, each large enough to hold a standard brown paper bag for glass, paper, plastic, or cans. Stackable plastic bins also can be used.

If your home has a basement or lower-level garage, consider installing separate chutes leading directly to receptacles on the lower level. If your kitchen and garage are on the same level and share a wall, you may be able to put in pass-throughs. Check your local building codes.

Baking

If making pastry is a passion, consider installing a baking center. The ideal location is between the oven and the refrigerator. You'll need at least 36 inches of work surface. A counter 3 to 6 inches lower than a standard counter is more comfortable for rolling out dough; a counter 30 inches deep leaves plenty of working room.

The baking center should include storage for cookbooks, mixing bowls, baking utensils, small appliances, baking pans, and staples such as flour, sugar, and spices. Handy features are tin-lined bread and flour drawers, a marble slab for rolling dough inset into a wood counter, a sink, and a wall-mounted scale for weighing ingredients.

▲ *Create a baking center by putting a work counter with base-cabinet storage close to the wall ovens.*

Fast Food

Mount a microwave oven near a refrigerator and above a 36-inch-wide counter to make a fast-food center that's ideal for heating and serving meals. Grouping these kitchen components close together helps kids take care of themselves without interfering in other kitchen activities.

➤ *Placing a microwave oven within kids' reach above a countertop near a refrigerator makes an ideal fast-food center.*

DESIGN DETAIL

■ Place the microwave oven approximately 42 inches off the floor.
■ To reduce the risk of burns, microwave ovens should be placed so you can slip hot dishes in and out without reaching or stretching too far.

■ If the primary users of a microwave oven are younger than 5, the interior should be even with or slightly lower than their shoulder.
■ For those older than 5, place the microwave so that heated food is no higher than 3 inches below shoulder height.

A Place for the Kitchen Table

With today's busy families eating on the run and often in shifts, an eating area in the kitchen is a big timesaver. If space is limited, consider converting one side of an island or peninsula into an eating counter. If you prefer more separation between workstation and table, consider a booth; it requires less area than a freestanding table and chairs. (Remember, though, booths are less convenient for seating and serving.)

No matter what form your dining table takes, allow each eater a 21- to 24-inch-long surface that's 15 inches deep.

Counter

Whether you call them breakfast bars, eating counters, or snack counters, this style of seating is the hallmark of a friendly kitchen.

■ A standard counter is 36 inches high and requires a 24-inch-high stool. If you put the eating counter at bar height (about 42 inches), you'll need a stool at least 30 inches high with a footrest 18 inches from the seat.
■ You'll need 24-inch-wide openings for knees.

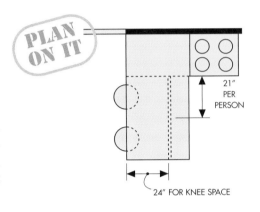

21"
PER
PERSON

24" FOR KNEE SPACE

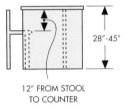

28"-45"

12" FROM STOOL
TO COUNTER

Booth

If your family dislikes countertop eating but there's no space for a dining table, build a booth.

■ Seating units should be as long as the table surface and allow 12 inches from seat to tabletop.
■ Install the seats so their front edges extend 3 or 4 inches under the table.

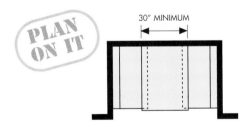

30" MINIMUM

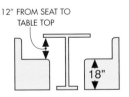

12" FROM SEAT TO
TABLE TOP

18"

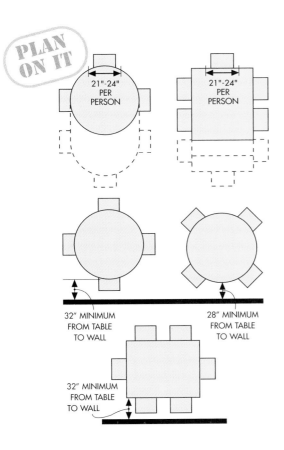

21"-24" PER PERSON

21"-24" PER PERSON

32" MINIMUM FROM TABLE TO WALL

28" MINIMUM FROM TABLE TO WALL

32" MINIMUM FROM TABLE TO WALL

Freestanding Table and Chairs

If you include a table and chairs in the kitchen, it's critical to allow enough room for comfortable dining, serving, and cleanup. Take note of these space requirements:

■ Plan 12 to 15 square feet of floor space for each diner; you'll need a minimum of 48 square feet to seat four.
■ Each person needs at least 21 inches of table space for comfortable dining.
■ A diner needs at least 32 inches to rise, and a server needs 44 inches of clearance to move around a table.
■ Move the table around to find the spot where chairs have the most room.
■ Be sure to include table extensions when deciding how much room you have and how many people you'll be able to serve at once.

To Do

Start a photo file.

To help visualize your new kitchen, start with a portfolio of photographs torn from the pages of favorite magazines. This portfolio of clippings helps you define your tastes and refine your ideas. Enhance your collection by making notes on the pictures. Carry the portfolio with you when you shop.

Doodle your ideas.

Start with a floor plan like the simple one on page 96. Architects typically draw floor plans to quarter scale (¼ inch equals 1 foot), but ½-inch scale requires less precision and may be easier to use. Draw an outline of the room on graph paper. (Make copies of the graph paper provided on page 109.) Lay a sheet of tracing paper over the outline and sketch elements such as cabinets and appliances. Use a clean sheet of tracing paper for each new idea.

Don't stop with a floor plan. Map the walls, too. That means drawing interior elevations—views of each wall showing the arrangements of cabinets, windows, and appliances (see the drawings on page 107).

Designed to Fit

Like tailored clothes, a custom-sized kitchen will fit better and be more comfortable. Countertop height, by way of example, can often make working in the kitchen less comfortable. If the countertop is too high, you might get sore neck muscles from lifting your shoulders to chop on the high countertop. If the countertop is too low, you may put unnecessary strain on your lower back by leaning over to work. Remodeling your kitchen is your opportunity to make the design fit. In design lingo—ergonomic design.

Most kitchen lifting involves taking out or putting away items kept in cabinets. Common sense says to store all items in a kitchen as close as possible to the point of first use. Weight is rarely a consideration. It should be. For many people, lifting is difficult. When you lift a 10-pound item with your arms fully extended there is a chance of losing control over that weight and having it fall. To avoid this, arrange your storage system so the heaviest items are kept in spaces between the hip and shoulder height, where they can be reached with the arms bent. This is also the range where the arm has the most leverage and experiences the least amount of stress. A nest of heavy mixing bowls, for example, should be kept in a drawer or roll-out shelf just below counter height. The same goes for dinnerware: It belongs in counter-level drawers not in overhead cabinets. Suggested measurements are shown on the following page and on page 30.

Store medium-weight items just above or below the heavy ones, but never higher than eye level or lower than the knees. The lightest items, such as cereal boxes, go in what many would consider the least accessible cabinets—those above the head or below the knees. Somewhat out of the way? Maybe. But a falling cereal box will not break your toe.

An added benefit is that children can reach what they need easily and safely. Dishes and flatware stored in drawers below the countertop are at a perfect height for the children to reach and take to the table.

Ergonomic design is not the same as universal design, a term used to describe a room designed to be accessible to a person in a wheelchair. But many aspects of universal, or barrier-free, design make life easier for everybody.

Kitchens designed for people in wheelchairs often have the dishwasher raised off the floor—a good idea for everyone because it eliminates bending and lifting. Yet kitchen designs often put the dishwasher under the counter. When the dishwasher is the primary appliance in an area intended for cleanup only, mounting it higher makes perfect ergonomic sense. Cabinets intended for wall ovens easily can be modified to enclose a raised dishwasher.

People in wheelchairs use counter backsplash areas for primary storage and limit what they keep in overhead cabinets. But most of us do the same thing without even thinking about it. Why? Because it's convenient. Items kept on the counter can be reached more easily than those stored anywhere else.

Take advantage of this natural tendency and build backsplash storage into at least one counter. An 8-inch-deep appliance garage behind tambours, or small shelf storage behind sliders, still leaves 15 inches of usable countertop. Another option is to plan one 36-inch-deep counter to provide a full 12 inches of backsplash storage without sacrificing any countertop work surface.

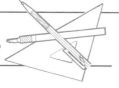

DESIGN DETAIL

■ A 30-inch height is recommended for children and seated users of tables or counters. Standard 36-inch counters work for people of average height. For taller people, counters should be between 42 and 45 inches high.

■ A built-in step that slides out from the toe-kick gives children a helpful boost up to a standard-height counter.

PUT LIGHT, EASY-TO-HANDLE
ITEMS IN HIGH CABINETS

KEEP ITEMS
WITHIN COMFORTABLE REACH.

EYE LEVEL
SHOULD DETERMINE
WINDOW HEIGHT.

STORE FREQUENTLY
USED ITEMS HERE

18" MINIMUM CLEARANCE
OVER COUNTER TOPS

24" MINIMUM CLEARANCE
OVER SINKS & RANGES

SHOULDER HEIGHT

HEAVIER ITEMS GO HERE
OR RIGHT UNDER COUNTER
FOR EASY LIFTING.

32 to 36" DEPENDING
ON USER'S HEIGHT

RARELY USED
ITEMS GO HERE

36" MINIMUM BETWEEN CABINETS

40" BETWEEN COUNTERS

48" BETWEEN APPLIANCES

IF CABINET DOORS AND APPLIANCES
FACE EACH OTHER, MAKE SURE TO
INCLUDE THE OPEN DOORS INTO YOUR
SPACE REQUIREMENTS.

Planning Review Checkpoints

Before proceeding to the next phase, take a moment to look over these final checkpoints to be sure your design is what you want.

✔ Be sure the kitchen allows direct access to all work centers.

✔ Make sure food preparation centers are outside of the normal in-and-out traffic flow.

✔ Plan sufficient counter space for tasks to be performed with the cook's natural work patterns in mind.

✔ Locate appliances at heights that work best for the physical characteristics of the cook.

✔ The working height of any appliance should be determined with safety in mind so food and utensils can be taken in or out safely.

✔ Plan different counter heights and different counter surfaces according to the tasks to be performed there, and to make using small appliances easier.

✔ Choose cabinet hardware and faucet handles that are designed to fit the individual's hand and muscle abilities.

FULL HEIGHT CABINET

✔ Know your cooking habits. If you regularly eat frozen, prepared meals, and you only like to shop once a week, pick a refrigerator with a large freezer.

10 Tips for a Better Kitchen

1. Think about how and where you use things in the kitchen so you can eliminate wasted steps. Store breakfast foods and bowls near the breakfast table. Duplicate frequently used spices and utensils so they are handy wherever you work. Keep wraps and plastic containers in one handy spot near a work surface for wrapping leftovers.

2. A second microwave oven and a mini refrigerator positioned at the edge of the kitchen work center will keep snackers out of the cook's way. Add a snack bar with stools for an afterschool spot for kids.

3. Make recycling easy. Equip a cupboard with stackable wire baskets for glass, metal, and plastic items. A separate drawer can conveniently house old newspapers. If you have a basement, consider installing chutes leading from the kitchen to separate receptacles below.

4. Think short. Placing the microwave oven at a height where kids can use it safely will not only ease your mind but your workload. For the same reason, put the kids' favorite dishes and snack foods on shelves they can reach.

5. Place a shelf beside or behind the range to keep cookbooks and cooking oils, a ceramic pot for utensils, and some spice jars handy. Place S hooks on the side of the range hood to hold frequently used pots and pans.

6. Tired of lugging water-filled stockpots from the sink to the cooktop? A swing-out tap, *right*, installed near the cooktop fills pots where you heat them. Or, install an extra-long hose on your sink's spray attachment.

7. Establish a message center near the kitchen telephone so your family can communicate. Put a bulletin board or blackboard on the wall, and store a calendar, notebooks, pens, and stick pins inside a nearby drawer.

8. Careful choices will help you cut kitchen cleaning time. Glass refrigerator shelves catch spills that wire ones let through. Flush-set or undermount sinks don't have a crumb-catching rim to worry about. Matte finishes don't show dirt as do high-gloss finishes.

9. Hang knives on a magnetic strip tacked to the backsplash. This makes it easy to spot the right size knife for a job and keeps sharp objects out of children's reach.

10. Install power strips with multiple plugs all along the backsplash so wherever you're working, you'll have the power you need.

Special-Order Kitchens

PHASE 3: Take a look at these to generate ideas for your dream kitchen.

The Bakery

The baker of this house, *right*, had a dream. She saw a light-filled, open space complete with large ovens, walls of cabinets, and an expanse of countertop, punctuated with a marble slab for rolling out dough. Her dream even included a fireplace for extra warmth.

The project design called for converting the former kitchen into a dining room, then remodeling the laundry, pantry, and project room into a large country kitchen. Working within the confines of the L-shaped room, the homeowners created a kitchen in one end of the L, and a bakery and sitting area around a table in the other end. A clerestory above the bakery lets in natural light as do French doors and the multipaned windows above a window seat. The dream is now a reality.

■ This kitchen features two separate work areas—one for baking and one for family meals.

■ A corner sink gives the cook two views: one of the family room and one to the outdoors.

■ Lots of cabinets hug one wall to provide storage for baking supplies, large cookie sheets, and cake pans.

■ A maple table serves as an oversize island for kitchen and bakery.

■ Open shelves keep kitchen gear handy and break up the long expanse of cabinetry.

■ The fireplace provides a focal point in the bakery.

> *The bakery brings in light to the rest of the kitchen, which features a massive refrigerator, a double corner sink, and butcher-block countertop. The bakery's counter has a marble slab inset.*

Perfect for Parties

The remodeled kitchen on these two pages was designed for parties—big and little ones, formal and casual ones. The renovation called for opening up the dinky kitchen to outdoor views, room for lots of people, a mini kitchen/wet bar, and generous food preparation areas.

The builder knocked out a partial wall between the kitchen and family room. He sealed off a powder room door, relocated the washer and dryer, bumped out the front wall for a sitting area, and repositioned the front door. The result is a gathering place that's also highly functional.

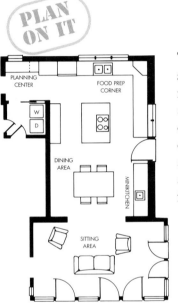

The new kitchen space and sitting room addition are open to each other and the outside patio, for a nonstop living area about 50 feet long.

▲ *Guests can help themselves here to hot and cold snacks and drinks, without disturbing the cook.*

➤ *The ovens stack next to the planning center because they aren't used for every meal.*

▼ *Terra-cotta floor tile and light-reflecting white surfaces—even on the sink and faucet—create a fresh, easy mood.*

◄ *Installing tall cabinets on an interior wall left spaces above the countertops for windows or art.*

Green Revolution

Reduce, reuse, recycle is the mantra of today's environmental movement. Nowhere is it more appropriate than in remodeling. By reducing waste, reusing materials, and recycling old houses, you're taking part in the green revolution.

Designing an earth-friendly renovation was priority number one for the people who own this kitchen. Not only did they save a historic house from the wrecking ball, but they also updated it using recycled materials. The kitchen floor, for example, is pine resawed out of old beams.

To get the light-filled, live-in kitchen they wanted, these homeowners converted their attached garage into livable space.
■ Above the work core of the new 14×18-foot kitchen is a two-story-high cathedral ceiling fitted with multipaned windows, flooding the kitchen with daylight.
■ One end of the core houses an Aga Cooker (a European design featuring several different ovens), the other a standard downdraft range—perfect for accommodating two cooks.
■ The cleanup center and professional-size refrigerator are positioned along the exterior wall between the two stations.
■ On the opposite wall, where the garage door once stood, full-length cabinets house cooking equipment and cookbooks. This is the planning center where menus are dreamed up.

◄ *Pine, resawed out of old beams, covers the floor in the breakfast area and in the work core.*

▲ *Painted beaded paneling ties in the new kitchen cabinets so they look as if they've always been part of the home. Across from the downdraft range, an Aga Cooker accommodates a second cook.*

THE RIGHT STUFF

When remodeling, consider these earth-friendly ideas:

■ Install energy-efficient windows. Coated glass panes keep heat in during winter months, and out during summer months. The glass costs a little more, but you can recoup the cost in energy savings, often in less than a year.

■ Cool naturally. Reposition windows to take advantage of natural breezes and cross ventilation. Equal-size windows on both windward and leeward sides of your house encourage breezes to move through. Install ceiling fans instead of air-conditioning.

■ Use nontoxic chemicals and paints. Biodegradable paint strippers and finishes are available in recyclable containers.

■ Salvage what you can. If there is nothing wrong with your old cabinets, instead of replacing them, refinish them. Search salvage yards for recycled building materials.

▼ Nooks, slots, and wire baskets provide a place to stash all kinds of kitchen stuff within easy reach.

➤ Sturdy pullouts raise shorter cooks to a more comfortable height.

Two Cooks

Two gung-ho cooks can bake and boil in the same kitchen without getting gummed up in the works. All it takes is attention to the basics of kitchen efficiency times two.

This kitchen remodeling shows how a little more floor space and a bit of strategic planning go a long way toward making a kitchen serve a cooking duo, plus cater to the kids.

PLAN ON IT

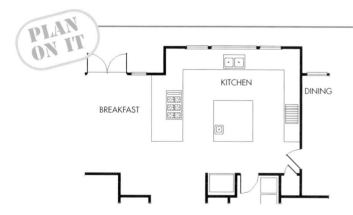

■ **Space.** To open up the space, the back wall was bumped out 8 feet and the wall between the breakfast room and family room was knocked out, thus changing a stop-and-go traffic pattern into a smooth road for two.

■ **Storage.** Storage and workstations were duplicated, and a center island with second sink added. The island is outfitted with an ensemble of storage niches and pullouts.
■ **Double vision.** The kitchen includes a cooktop peninsula, indoor barbecue grill, two sinks, and three ovens.
■ **Style.** Crown molding, paneled cabinets, 1×6-inch ceiling paneling, and period light fixtures enhance the country kitchen style. Glass-front cabinets add to the openness.
■ **Lighting.** An arched window was added to admit more sun. Pendant lights installed at the workstations illuminate each task.

▲ *Once a dreary place, the kitchen now boasts lots of counter space and windows.*

Do-It-Yourself Family

When the cost of their dream kitchen exceeded their expectations, these homeowners decided to go for it and do the remodeling themselves. One expense they did make was hiring a designer to lay out the basics; then they spent two years reworking the plans as their tastes and the space evolved. Once they were comfortable with the design, they gutted the room.

Now the kitchen is light, bright, and functional. A spacious island serves as the centerpiece. Equipped with a sink, it makes room for up to six cooks around it.

One end of the island cradles as much as three cases of wine; the other end hides the microwave oven. Though they designed the cabinetry themselves, the homeowners hired a cabinetmaker to build the units.

■ The island divides the kitchen into work areas. One, equipped with a double sink, serves as a food preparation/cleanup area. The other work area focuses on cooking, with easy access to the range, refrigerator, and a vegetable sink in the island.

■ An alcove opposite the sink provides space for a vintage range and a refrigerator. Spice storage along one wall of the refrigerator takes advantage of between-stud space. Storage above the refrigerator corrals cookbooks.

■ The refrigerator, positioned at one side of the kitchen, lets kids grab a snack without interfering with the cook.

■ The microwave oven is tucked out of sight at the end of the island where it's a handy stop between the refrigerator and table. This below-counter location makes it safer for kids to use.

■ A built-in dining nook takes up less space than a table and chairs and provides storage for linens and dinnerware in the benches.

■ A bump-out in the former breakfast room provides a spot for a full-size washer and dryer.

continued

◄ *Walls vanished to make room for windows in this light, bright kitchen. The homeowners chose a basic, snappy black-and-white scheme with wide appeal.*

Decorating Ideas

The Right White
There are many shades of white, each with its own subtle appeal. Yellow and cream-base whites work well with earth tones. When the palette is cool, however, choose whites with pink or peach undertones.

Choosing the off-white that best complements a color scheme also is important. If you're doing a room with periwinkle furnishings, for example, you should find an off-white with a hint of periwinkle.

The best way to choose the right white is to test it in your home. Many manufacturers are now making paint chips as large as 5×7 inches. Take these larger chips home, place them vertically against the wall, and observe them in the lighting conditions of the room at varying times. A white may look startlingly different in the day than at night. If you have swatches of fabrics or other items you'll use in that space, view the whites beside them as well. Color can reflect upon color.

Elements of the Family Kitchen

■ Go for the highest quality paint job on white cabinets for easy cleaning and durability.

■ Include a work area just so the kids can help. Cutting the work table down to 3 inches below standard will give them easier access.

■ If children will be using the microwave oven, place it where they can comfortably reach it, and include a nearby counter for setting down hot dishes.

■ Choose a fairly soft, comfortable material for floors. Wood is good; it cleans easily, and dishes are less likely to break when dropped.

■ Choose furnishings that can take abuse or that will age nicely.

■ Go for rounded edges on countertops and easy-to-reach cabinetry shelves.

■ Depending on how you live, organize your kitchen area for different activities. Consider the ages of your children and what their needs are. Will the children do homework in the kitchen? Does the family congregate in the kitchen? For example, you may want three areas—one for preparation, one for eating, and one for play.

▲ *Because this is a vintage kitchen, the microwave is hidden at the end of the island where its high-tech personality is not easily seen.*

Experts' Insight

If you're doing the remodeling work yourself, pay attention to these tips:

■ Don't underestimate the amount of time it will take to do a job. Typically, do-it-yourselfers plan three times more work than they can complete in a weekend.

■ Spouses should plan work together, drawing on each other's strengths. One person often is more of a planner and organizer; the other might be good at carrying out tasks.

■ Brainstorm before each work session. You'll be able to solve problems before they arise.

■ Know what you want. Study magazines, tear out photographs of rooms you like, and keep a folder of your favorites.

■ Finish your initial design, then wait a year. Plans evolve, getting better and better.

■ Search around before hiring people. You don't need to settle for expensive prices. You might want to do some of the work yourself, recycle items, or shop for better prices on appliances and materials.

■ Keep your home comfortable while you remodel. Clean up clutter every day and store tools and supplies out of sight.

■ When you're remodeling an existing space, don't expect perfection. Some problems can't be solved without major expense, so be prepared to spend more or let an item go.

> ▶ *A side-by-side refrigerator slips into a nook trimmed with molding to achieve the look of cabinetry.*

> ▼ *Bifold doors help conceal any mess in this hideaway laundry center. Glass panes in the upper panels allow light to flow into the kitchen.*

Visit Kitchens

Nothing helps you imagine your kitchen project more than seeing the elements you're considering in real life. Ask to see projects of the architect, builder, or designer you may be working with. When you visit, ask the current residents how they like their kitchen.

Family and friends may know of a kitchen like the one you're considering. Visit model homes in new housing developments, and watch for home tours in your area. These can show you how different design and decorating elements look in real life, and you might find a kitchen design you'd like to emulate.

Remodeling Strategies

PHASE 4: Set your strategy—choose from cabinet makeovers to moving walls.

The time you've spent using and analyzing your present kitchen in terms of how it functions probably has given you a good sense of what it needs to be more efficient and comfortable. You also should have a good idea of the basic design and the extent of your project.

Now it's time to nail down your solutions, whether they're purely cosmetic or wholesale changes of space. This chapter will give you advice on carrying out your project, including estimating costs.

▲ *Reworking the layout and adding new cabinets and finishes made this kitchen more modern and efficient. There's even room to sit and plan.*

➤ *Opening the wall to the dining room connected the kitchen and eating areas into one flowing space. The homeowner handled demolition himself and served as general contractor. Total remodeling cost was $13,380.*

Cabinet Makeover

If you like everything about your kitchen except the way it looks, consider yourself lucky. Few kitchens of middle or advanced age satisfy today's design standards. Fewer still won't benefit from a style update. So if you have the space and layout you need, you may only need to renew surfaces to give the room a fresh, new look.

If you're really fortunate, you won't even have to replace the cabinets. You can paint them or reface them instead. As the name implies, refacing is a surface change accomplished by adding a layer of wood veneer or plastic laminate to the cabinet body. New cabinet doors, drawer fronts, hinges, and hardware then are added. Refacing can transform dreary, out-of-date cabinets into fresh ones. Your old cabinets will be new again.

A major benefit of refacing is that it causes only minimum disruption of the house and family routine. In some cases, it's not even necessary to empty the cabinets. Important, too, for do-it-yourselfers is that this work can be done piecemeal, in your spare time.

There is more than one way to get the refacing done. Flip through the Yellow Pages of your telephone book under "Kitchen Cabinets," and you're likely to find services specializing in cabinet refacing. On the first visit to your home, workers record the dimensions of all your cabinets, doors, and drawers. On the second visit, they reface the cabinets and install whatever new parts you've decided on, all for thousands of dollars less than the cost of new cabinets.

If you're committed to doing the work yourself and willing to devote several weekends to the project, refacing can be accomplished with quality, low-cost, ready-to-install materials available at most home centers. However, chances are you'll find only a few styles available, compared to several options offered by a refacing service. Also, if your kitchen contains lots of custom dimensions, it may be difficult to make off-the-shelf products fit. In an average-size kitchen, expect to spend $1,000 to $1,500 for cabinet refacing materials.

Another do-it-yourself option is to have doors and drawer fronts custom-made by a local mill-worker, then reface remaining cabinet surfaces yourself. Though more expensive than store-bought refacing systems, millworkers offer a range of style options that will fit precisely to any size custom cabinetry you have, and you'll get a quality job.

However you go about refacing your cabinets, take this opportunity to renovate the insides as well. Old cabinets can be fitted with the latest in storage hardware, such as sliders for shelving, roll-out bins for pots and baking pans, door-mounted garbage bins with self-closing lids, and swing-up platforms for small appliances. It may be possible to change a cabinet with doors into one with a bank of drawers. Or, two narrow drawers may be combined to make one that is wider and more useful. If you have extra space, consider adding new matching cabinets. Maybe a wall cabinet can be reconfigured to house a microwave oven.

➤ *Laminate countertops and homemade window treatments helped stretch the homeowners' budget.*

▼ *This older kitchen got a brand-new, lighter look from a cabinet-refacing system.*

PROBLEM SOLUTION

This kitchen, *above*, was remodeled by a do-it-yourselfer on a lean budget. The homeowner decided to keep the sink, faucet, and refrigerator because they worked and still looked good. On the other hand, the dishwasher was broken and a brown finish doomed the double ovens. In addition, the remodeler needed to replace the countertops. Although the cabinets were in good condition, a dated door style and dark stain made them a poor design element.

Using an inexpensive cabinet refacing system (a total of $1,050), the homeowner replaced old cabinet doors and drawer fronts with new ones made of red oak and refaced the cabinet bodies with a matching veneer. A white stain rubbed over the wood creates pink highlights while permitting the grain to show through. A new crown molding across the top completes the cabinets' transformation. Total cost for remodeling the kitchen: $3,635.

Kitchen Face-Lift

Next to refacing or painting cabinetry, giving your kitchen a face-lift is the most inexpensive remodeling strategy. Face-lifting entails new surfaces—flooring, countertops, walls, the ceiling—as well as new appliances, light fixtures, and the sink and faucet. Face-lifting is an option when you're happy with the amount of space you have and the layout, but you just want to update the look and durability. It's also a project you may be able to do all or part of yourself, saving money in the process.

As for other rooms, there are unlimited options for paint and wall coverings to spruce up the walls; just make sure whatever you choose can be easily cleaned. Window treatments also are diverse, but for ease of installation and cleaning, keep the setups uncomplicated.

Old countertops can be unfastened and removed from their base cabinets; the measurements for new surfaces will stay the same. New counters also can be reshaped and resized to improve their appearance and function.

New flooring is definitely a do-it-yourself option, especially if you choose vinyl or linoleum. Wood is a popular kitchen flooring choice, thanks to improvements in protective coatings.

Finally, consider replacing sinks, faucets, lighting, and appliances as part of a total makeover. If these items are more than 10 years old, they're probably showing signs of wear and may not have some of the convenience and operating features today's products offer.

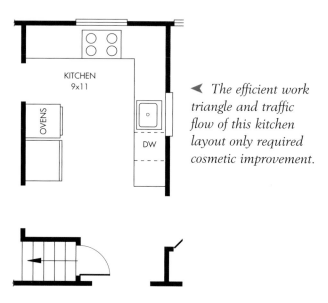

◄ The efficient work triangle and traffic flow of this kitchen layout only required cosmetic improvement.

PROBLEM ? SOLUTION

New owners transformed a dark, inefficient, little L-shaped kitchen sticky from years of grime into an attractive, classic kitchen they could show with pride.

To achieve their goals on a modest budget, they substituted their own labor when they could. Not only did they design the remodeling themselves, they acted as general contractor, scheduling subcontractors. For things that had to look finished, they hired professional help.

Work that wouldn't show, and they were qualified to do, they did themselves.

Working together, they tore out cabinets, scoured kitchen walls, pried up linoleum, and scraped glue off the subfloor. They replumbed the kitchen and ran wiring to the porch, calling in a professional to hook up the switches and outlets and handle tricky rewiring. They ordered custom cabinets and had them professionally installed to ensure precise alignment.

➤ *New surfaces, lighting, and appliances gave this once-dreary kitchen a whole new look.*

▼ *Custom cabinets duplicate the molding of the window above the range, carrying it across the room in a sleek unbroken line; the black-and-white floor sports a vintage pattern.*

Rethinking Layout

In the real world, kitchens can have all kinds of layout quirks. They can turn one or more corners, zigging one way, then zagging another. They can be broken up by too many doorways, creating both traffic problems and abbreviated cabinet and counter runs. Some kitchens are underequipped with blank wall sections where cabinets and counters should be. Others, especially in older houses, are completely cut off from other rooms or have just a few small windows. Each of these layout problems has a remodeling solution.

If too many doorways are a problem, look for one to close off, especially if it allows for a continuous run of cabinets and counters. Sometimes a doorway to another room can be moved to a wall outside the kitchen. Moving a door a few feet, even inches, may be enough of a solution. It may be difficult to close off an exterior door, but it might be possible to shift it elsewhere.

If deep windows are getting in the way of a cabinet or counter you'd like to add, the fix is simple: Put in a smaller window with a higher sill—at least 42 inches high for adequate clearance over a 36-inch counter. Windows that are too small can be replaced by larger ones, providing better lighting and views. Windows can even be installed into the backsplash or high over the tops of wall cabinets.

When a kitchen is isolated from an eating area, be it a breakfast zone or a formal dining room, a pass-through may be the best way to increase communication between the two. This is basically a nicely finished space in the wall connecting two rooms, making them both feel larger.

A kitchen that turns one corner too many is a special problem; straightening it out may require reshaping an adjacent room. Consider taking square footage from that room and giving it to the kitchen.

Obviously, one of the easiest remodeling strategies is filling in blank space. A one-wall kitchen could become an L; an L-shaped kitchen could gain a leg and become a U. Or, there might be space to add an island or peninsula.

If your new layout involves moving fixtures and appliances, make sure your plans stay within the local building code. There may also be minimum requirements for electrical outlets along the backsplash. Before you get too far along in your planning and budgeting, it's wise to get input from a building inspector.

The 1920s kitchen on the facing page incorporates these features:

■ A six-burner cooktop sits between two chimneys. Below the cooktop, oversize drawers keep pots and pans handy with no stacking.

■ Adjacent to the cooktop, tile counters provide spots for setting hot pots. Dark green laminate adds color at an affordable price.

■ The cabinetry has traditional panel construction, cupped reproduction pulls, and glass.

◄ *Large floor geometrics jazz up this otherwise traditional kitchen.*

▲ *New windows over the eating booth provide lots of sunlight and a view of the garden.*

▲ *This desk area took the place of an eating area. A laminate countertop was extended from the base cabinet to the wall.*

◄ This small cooking alcove holds the refrigerator, storage for cookware, full-size sink, and professional range.

Annex Adjacent Space

If your kitchen is cramped for space, look to surrounding areas, such as a porch, utility room, or pantry for room to grow. Maybe a little-used formal dining room would be more functional as a connected eat-in area, or it could contribute to making the kitchen larger.

So, if you need more space, the first question is: What's on the other side of the walls that have the kitchen hemmed in? Next question: Is that adjacent space, the way it currently functions, really essential to your lifestyle?

Since the area you're eyeing is not likely to be totally unused, you have to decide if its function can be ended, changed, or achieved with less space. Also, in order to annex all or part of an adjacent space, you may have to include its function into your kitchen-to-be. In the case of a pantry, breakfast nook, or dining area, that can be easy. If the adjacent area is a utility room, mudroom, or laundry, you may have a greater challenge relocating the coveted space's function.

Assuming that some adjacent space is available, how do you assimilate it into your kitchen? In most cases, you don't. Instead, you treat the combined space as an entirely new area, giving you the opportunity to completely rearrange your kitchen and add more storage, counter space, and other features.

With that kind of fresh-start approach, you'll need to sit down and list all the things you want your kitchen to have, in order of their importance. After that, you'll have the tough task of space allocation. Although you've added square footage by annexation, you won't know if your dream kitchen will fit your real space until you've taken all the measurements and worked out the details on paper, as described in Phase 7. There is no way to eyeball a job like this.

One of the hardest obstacles to overcome in looking at a newly formed space is a tendency to think of your kitchen as it exists now, only larger. Unless you intend to retain the core layout and simply expand the storage or eating spaces, forget about your present kitchen. Start over working through several possibilities—there's never just one way to design a room.

➤ With its zigzagging counters and sunny, open space, this remade kitchen lends itself to team cooking and cleanup plus relaxed eating.

PROBLEM ? SOLUTION

Before remodeling, the layout of this kitchen was barely adequate for a single cook. The homeowners, both cooks, needed an open plan with room for their children. They also wanted yard access for grilling and eating outside.

To open up the area, they combined the kitchen, breakfast, and entry areas into one large room. To pick up yard space, they shaved off a slender bump-out (added by previous owners) and added a new patio and entry. When the dust cleared, they had created a 450-square-foot space with lots of friendly spots for cooking, eating, and relaxing.

The space works as a series of versatile activity stations. For example, a snack area, equipped with a microwave oven, is built into the island.

In redesigning the kitchen, the couple restored the original Tudor flavor of the house, replacing stainless-steel appliances and slick finishes with old-fashioned cabinets and mellow wood floors. They carefully stripped off all the old window and door moldings before demolition and reused them. They also recycled original lead-glass doors and used them as fronts for a stereo-television hutch.

Build an Addition

If the possibilities for gaining space internally won't work, and you don't want to make do with a small kitchen, you have the option of adding on. Most families don't consider an addition because of the time and expense involved, but those who do, find they usually gain more than just the kitchen they've always wanted. The new kitchen often comes hand in hand with a family room, a larger and more conveniently located dining space, or architectural improvements that can make a home more livable.

When an addition begins to evolve from a dream to a strong possibility, it's time to think through what you want the new space to do.

■ **How much space can you afford?** A common range for a contractor-built addition is $50 to $100 a square foot. Square-foot materials for a do-it-yourself project range from $25 to $50.

■ **Should you move a wall?** Consider whether you should move out the exterior kitchen wall or involve other areas of the house as well.

■ **Will your kitchen stay where it is and expand?** Or will it relocate to another part of the house?

■ **Where can you expand?** Limitations may be more than just physical if you want to build beyond setback or other zoning requirements.

■ **What functions do you want the addition to perform?** More functions need more space, but be aware that cost per square foot decreases as the addition gets larger.

■ **Do you want your kitchen to do something it couldn't do before?** This is the most important consideration. No one knows your kitchen better than you, so you're the expert when it comes to analyzing its strengths and its flaws.

Don't limit your planning exclusively to the kitchen. Play with some plans on paper. For instance, add the dining table and indicate the furnishings you'll want in an eat-in area. When you've earmarked so much space per function, settle down to the business of laying out your kitchen with just the right arrangement of work centers and storage.

At this point it makes a lot of sense to call in a professional designer. Building an addition is a big investment of time and money. Getting the design just right is top priority.

Add a Breakfast Bay

You don't have to add lots of square footage to get functional space. In this kitchen, a sunny bay window gives a once-windowless kitchen a fresh outlook, plus eat-in space.

◄ *A dreary mudroom once kept this kitchen in the dark. Now the sun pours in all day—even through the ceiling. The addition also makes room for an eating area.*

➤ *Square-mullioned transoms stretch this bay window to the eaves.*

▲ *Changes in shapes, surfaces, and levels keep this kitchen interesting and more functional.*

◀ *About 10½ feet wide on each side, the bay area of the addition is just large enough to accommodate talking and quiet activity.*

Experts' Insight

Adding a family space doesn't always require a traditional room addition. The kitchen, *above*, was extended, then broken out of its box shape with an angled bay. A total of 230 square feet was added. The homeowners offer this advice:

■ Be clear about your goals. They wanted a family kitchen, not a family room, and that's just what they got. Set priorities, and stay focused on your needs.

■ Merge old spaces with new. Avoid mental boundaries based on the old floor plan. This plan uses an island that cuts through the middle of the space, zoning the kitchen into work, sitting, dining, and planning areas.

■ Consider a bay to build interest while expanding the living area. Here the bay was part of a larger addition, but at your house, a bay could be all the space you need.

■ Use seating benches or a built-in banquette for comfortable seating in a small space.

■ Conserve space by packing all the function you can into an island. This island, for example, serves as a cooking area, snack bar, and storage spot—and includes a media center facing the sitting area.

Estimating Costs

Budget often dictates reality. It's important right from the beginning to consider how much your remodeling will cost. By setting a fixed price, then trying to meet it, you'll be more aware of getting the most for your dollar.

A good rule of thumb is to spend about 10 to 15 percent of your home's value on a kitchen remodeling, because typically you will be able to make that much back when you sell. If the job is professionally designed and built, you can expect to reap a 94% return for a major kitchen remodeling that moves walls and plumbing and a 104% return for a minor kitchen remodeling.

Trying to estimate even average costs for a remodeling project is difficult because no two jobs are alike. Seemingly small differences in critical details such as materials and placement of appliances can lead to big cost variations.

But do-it-yourselfers and contractors alike have to start their budgeting somewhere, and to help them out there are several estimating guides covering just about every aspect of home building and remodeling. The R.S. Means Company publishes several of them. Their *Interior Home Improvement Costs* (1994, $19.95) gives material, labor, and cost breakdowns for more than a dozen different kinds of kitchens. No matter what your kitchen looks like, this reference guide will help you estimate costs for the remodelings in this book.

According to the latest trends survey in 1994 by the National Kitchen and Bath Association, the average price of a remodeled kitchen is $17,360. Percentages of dollars spent break out this way:

Labor	21%	Lighting	3%
Flooring	4%	Appliances	8%
Cabinets	43%	Fixtures	5%
Countertops	12%	Other	4%

◄ *Nothing delivers dramatic punch like a checkerboard floor, but how much will it cost? It all depends on what type of checkers you're playing with. Quality 12×12-inch vinyl square tiles like these cost $2 to $3 per square foot. Ceramic tile costs $6 to $7 per square foot. For marble, you'll pay $15 to $17 per square foot, plus the installation fees.*

Creating a Budget

Make a list of the problems your kitchen presents and the enhancements you want to make. Your kitchen project probably will take elements from most or all of the remodelings in this book.

Keep in mind that the fewer structural changes you make, the easier it will be on the budget. If possible, don't move the location of your sink or a gas appliance. Running new supply lines can be expensive.

Also, study appliances and materials of countertops and flooring to ensure quality but keep your costs within your budget.

Sample Estimator

This basic 9½×13-foot peninsula kitchen reflects material prices for stock cabinetry, standard appliances, and laminate countertops. Vinyl flooring is midpriced at about $4 a foot. Ask your contractor about per-hour labor costs and apply them to the hours each job will take. The standard cost for this kitchen is $12,850 (includes contractor's fee and materials).

Description	Labor (in hours)	Material (in $)
Flooring, vinyl sheet goods to cover 100 square feet	5	465
Wall cabinets, 34 linear feet, 12 inches deep, hardwood	10	1,395
Base cabinets, 29 linear feet, 12 inches deep, hardwood	11	2,501
Laminate countertop with backsplash, 32 linear feet	8	330
Stock cornice molding trim	2	52
Paint trim, ceilings, and wall	6	68
Built-in cooking range, 30 inches wide, 1 oven	4	424
2-speed vented range hood	4	36
19-cubic-foot frost-free refrigerator	2	726
Stainless-steel double-bowl sink with faucets, 33×22 inches	6	371
2-cycle built-in dishwasher	8	325
Rough-in supply, waste, and vent for sink and dishwasher	18	160
Totals	84	$6,853

Sure Cures for Floor Plans

If you block a doorway when you open the refrigerator, if you stumble over the kids while preparing dinner, if opening the dishwasher blocks access to the cabinet where dishes are stored, you've experienced the frustration of a poor floor plan. Don't just live with the problem; fix it. It may not be as difficult as you think. Some commonsense cures include:

Protect the Work Area
Avoid collisions and interruptions by routing traffic around the work triangle (the area connecting the refrigerator, sink, and cooktop) whenever it is possible.

Design Strategic Storage
Minimal storage standards call for 18 square feet of cabinet space, plus 6 additional square feet for each family member. Store items near their area of first use: dishes close to the table, pans near the range, and staples close to the baking center and food-preparation area.

Install Counters Near Work Sites
Flank the sink with plenty of counter space; 30 to 36 inches on each side is ideal. Put a 15-inch counter on the handle side of the refrigerator and 15 to 18 inches on either side of the cooktop for storing or setting condiments, cutting boards, and other paraphernalia.

Include Eating Space
Allow at least 32 inches between the table and a wall. In a small kitchen, let a counter double as a food-preparation and serving surface.

Allow Space Between Work Centers
Guidelines call for 4 to 9 feet between the range and refrigerator, 4 to 7 feet between the refrigerator and sink, and 4 to 6 feet between the sink and range. Less space causes congestion; more creates useless steps.

Add an Island

Before
A large work triangle created extra steps and wasted floor space. Traffic cut through the work area disrupting food preparation.

After
■ Placing the cooktop in an island establishes a more efficient work triangle. Appliances, countertops, and storage occupy an L-shaped area.
■ The island separates the work area from the traffic flow, yields additional storage space, and provides a spot for eating in the kitchen.

■ Relocating the range frees up space for a planning or study center away from the work triangle.
■ Retaining the original location of the sink minimizes plumbing changes (and cost) and preserves the view.

Before   After

Rework Traffic Flow

Before
Crowded into one corner, the work area lacked natural light and usable counter space.

After
■ Relocating two doorways and annexing the original porch improves traffic flow and makes room for a laundry area tucked behind bifold doors.
■ A closet accessed from the hall provides storage for coats and backpacks. The new closet makes the refrigerator appear built in.

■ A peninsula running through the middle of the kitchen separates the work area and traffic flow and provides counter and dining space.

Before   After

Rework the Layout

Before
This kitchen had three inconvenient doorways. Small windows over the sink and eating nook didn't bring in enough natural light. The refrigerator was inconveniently placed outside the main work area, and fixed benches in the eating nook were neither practical nor comfortable.

After
■ Sliding glass doors replace two small doors at one end of the kitchen, bringing in lots of natural light and backyard views.
■ Moving the sink a little to the right allows room for the refrigerator on the same wall.

■ Replacing the range with a cooktop forms an efficient work triangle and the oven, used less often, doesn't interfere with the main work area.
■ Three windows over the sink and new peninsula invite in plenty of sunshine.
■ Cushioned chairs on casters provide comfortable seating at the counter, and they easily roll to the planning desk when needed.

Before   After

Rework a Corridor

Before
The family had to troop through the kitchen just to get outside. Neither the cooktop nor the refrigerator had any nearby counter space. The kitchen lacked eating space.

After
■ Reworking the entry provides an alternate route outside and cuts down on traffic through the kitchen.
■ A bump-out over the sink makes the work core of the kitchen feel larger.
■ An L-shaped work area on one side of the kitchen protects the cooktop from traffic inter-

ference and provides counter space next to the refrigerator and cooktop.
■ Built-in benches take up less room than chairs and make space for a kitchen eating area.

Before   After

continued

Annex Space

Before

At only 7 feet wide, the dining room crowded diners. The adjacent kitchen, also 7 feet wide, served as a traffic route with three doorways. Appliances and sink were scattered.

After

■ Removing the wall between kitchen and dining room and closing up a dining room doorway makes way for an efficient U-shaped kitchen.

■ To preserve the windows in the original dining room, the sink occupies the wall opposite the range, and a counter stretches past the windows.

■ A bump-out on one side of the new breakfast area provides room for a table and chairs.

■ Traffic flows around the breakfast area rather than through the kitchen.

Before   **After**

Take Down the Walls

Before

Traffic coming in the garage door traveled right through the work core and out the back door. The kitchen and the dining room were both so small they made the family feel claustrophobic.

After

■ Removing the wall between the kitchen and dining room opens up the space and makes room for a peninsula.

■ A change in traffic routes eliminates travel through the work triangle.

■ A partial wall helps the refrigerator appear built-in.

■ In the dining area, a new door provides access to a deck, and a built-in buffet adds storage for tableware and a serving counter for entertaining.

Before   **After**

Build an Addition

Before

Poor design forced the cook to hike to the refrigerator and channeled traffic into the work area. Too little counter space made cooking difficult.

After

■ An addition creates a single room for cooking, eating, and relaxing.

■ The L-shaped island diverts traffic from the work core and makes space for the cooktop and an extra sink.

■ The primary sink, cooktop, and refrigerator form an efficient work area. The small sink, refrigerator, and microwave oven comprise a second work triangle near the family room.

Before   **After**

Help!

Building and remodeling professionals make a living out of seeing the possibilities in a place. You'll pay for their expertise, but if it prevents you from making a costly mistake and gets you the best kitchen, it's well worth the price. Use the following resources.

Architect—An architect is a good choice if you're planning an addition or an extensive remodeling. An architect can design the structure for your new kitchen to fit all your needs and oversee the construction.

Building designer—A building designer may be a better choice than an architect if your job is not extensive. Building designers are more specialized and usually less expensive than architects. They are capable of customizing existing plans.

Certified Kitchen Designer—A Certified Kitchen Designer (CKD) focuses on how the space works. A CKD will examine your lifestyle and come up with a design that suits it. Although not as qualified as an architect for complex plans, a CKD can perform most similar services at less cost.

Interior designer—An interior designer offers a variety of services, from designing an entire project to decorating and adding the final touches to make that functional kitchen attractive. An interior designer also can act as a liaison between you and your subcontractors.

Numbers to Know

Often the best way to find the right professional is word of mouth. Survey neighbors, friends, and family to find out who they have used. If that doesn't produce a list of professionals and you don't want to just grab a name out of the Yellow Pages, consult one of the following organizations.

■ **The American Institute of Architects.** The AIA offers a complete homeowner package, including worksheets, a video, and a booklet on selecting an architect. For information, call your local chapter or the national headquarters in Washington, D.C., at 202/626-7572.

■ **National Kitchen and Bath Association.** The NKBA, publishes a free directory listing all CKDs. Call 908/852-0033 between 9 a.m. and 5 p.m. Eastern Standard Time.

■ **The American Society of Interior Designers.** ASID provides a free Client/Designer Selection Service. The group will list the names of several designers best suited for your plan and your budget. Call 800/775-2743 between 10 a.m. and 6 p.m. Eastern Standard Time.

■ **The National Association of Home Builders.** The NAHB Remodelor's Council publishes a free 12-page booklet on choosing a reputable builder. Request the free booklet by sending a self-addressed, stamped envelope to NAHB Remodelor's Council, 1201 15th St., NW, Washington, DC 20005.

TOOLS TO USE

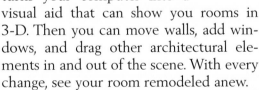

If your mind can't visualize the results of a remodeling, maybe your computer can. Computer-aided design (CAD) software turns your computer into a visual aid that can show you rooms in 3-D. Then you can move walls, add windows, and drag other architectural elements in and out of the scene. With every change, see your room remodeled anew.

Buying this software makes sense if you enjoy creating on the computer and if you need to do some serious planning. Shop carefully; some software packages are much easier to use than others. For example, some packages include a standard library of kitchen elements such as sinks and cabinets. Others ask you to draw your own or purchase them separately.

Selecting Materials

PHASE 5: Now move to specific choices: What materials fit your style and needs?

In the long run, proper selection of materials can save a lot of money on the cost of a large remodeling project. There are times when buying only the best materials will pay off, but there also are times when less expensive materials will get the job done without sacrificing appearance or long-lasting quality. Above all, when selecting materials think durability and maintenance.

▲ *Sometimes choices of materials can make a big visual difference. In small kitchens judicious use of mirrors can make rooms appear larger. The backsplash and upper cabinets of this bar area are lined with mirrors to create the illusion of greater depth even with an icemaker, ideal for serving guests, and a second sink in the small area.*

Here's how this kitchen works:
- A large center island provides a spot for children and guests without getting in the way of the cook.
- In the corner between the sink and the cooktop special cabinets were used to house a small TV.
- A closet by the kitchen's back door keeps the children's coats and school gear off the floor and out of sight.
- Non-intrusive light fixtures were chosen to keep the lines of the kitchen simple. Recessed downlights provide bright, overall lighting, and under-cabinet lights brighten work surfaces.

▲ *Choosing sunshine yellow walls and cool white cabinetry made this remodeled kitchen look as fresh as starched cotton. The white tile floor is inset with green diamonds to match the granite-topped island.*

▲ *In this remodeling, the appliances were left in place but the cabinets underwent a face-lift. They received new maple cabinet frames with blue laminate panels that accentuate the mellow pine of the farmhouse-style table and chairs. The blue of the laminate is repeated in a band of trim at the ceiling. A lower, wider band of trim on the ceiling was painted mahogany red for contrast.*

Cabinets

Because cabinetry is the largest element in the kitchen, it does the most to establish your room's style. Sleek slab doors with no exposed hardware create the clean lines of contemporary design. An open plate rack and knotty wood convey a casual country feel. Glass, mullioned cabinet doors, elaborate moldings, and glass knobs provide a traditional look.

Remember, though, that cabinetry not only has the biggest impact on the look of a new kitchen, but it also takes the biggest bite out of your budget. With that much at stake, it's important to study your options before you buy.

The Frame Game

The choices in cabinetry construction—frame or frameless—are easy to spot. Frameless cabinetry features a continuous surface of doors and drawer fronts. On frame cabinets, the exposed edges of the frame, called the reveal, show around doors and drawers. There are other differences as well.

■ The biggest advantage of *frame cabinets* is their stability. The back, bottom, top, and sides of a cabinet can be constructed from thinner material because the frame gives the whole body support.

A disadvantage is the space taken up by the frame. Door and drawer openings are smaller on frame cabinets than on frameless units. As a result, drawers and roll-out accessories will be smaller than the overall width of the cabinet.

■ The main advantages of *frameless cabinets* are accessibility and style. With no frame to steal or impinge on space, the cabinets open up to their full potential. And with no frame showing, the cabinets present a clean, simple design.

One disadvantage is that planning a layout with frameless units requires expertise. It's important to allow door clearances that may not be needed with framed units. Also, fillers are needed when one cabinet is installed at an angle to another.

Stock or Custom

When it comes to the way cabinets are manufactured, there are four categories: stock, semicustom, custom, and ready-to-assemble.

■ **Stock** cabinetry is an inexpensive alternative, but it also has the fewest features. You've probably seen these for sale in lumberyards and home centers. The manufacturing method necessitates standardization of sizes and surface finishes.

The smallest cabinet is 9 inches wide; the largest 48 inches wide. The units increase in size by 3-inch increments. Door position is also standard. Cabinets less than 24 inches wide have one door; those wider have two. Interior fittings, such as lazy Susans and pullout shelves, cost extra.

■ **Semicustom** cabinets are built by a manufacturer to fit your kitchen. You specify sizes and interior fittings. Be aware that some manufacturers of semicustom cabinetry do not offer much more variation in size than preassembled stock cabinets. Still, you are likely to have more selections in door styles and finishes. There may be added cost for a special finish.

■ **Custom** cabinetry offers the advantage of special sizes, unusual door designs, custom finishes, and interior fittings. For example, you can specify extra height for base cabinets if you are tall and extra depth if you need additional countertop or storage space. Built on-site, custom cabinets are the most expensive and require the most time from ordering to installation.

■ **Ready-to-assemble (RTA)** cabinets fall at the other end of the cost spectrum. They include all the parts and assembly hardware and require several hours of your time with a screwdriver or wrench and maybe a drill. RTA lines won't have the range of styles that stock and custom stock brands offer, but they will be quite current and carry attractive price tags.

Undercover Agents

When it comes to what cabinets are made of, there's a lot going on under the surface. The material under the cabinet surface, often called the substrate, makes a big difference in the quality of the cabinets. Wood cabinets, for instance, are made of a variety of wood products and veneers. Solid wood is used only in doors and frames, if at all. The main component of cabinetry will be plywood or a type of particleboard.

■ **Particleboard** is made from wood particles mixed with resin and bonded under pressure. It serves as the base for most laminate and as hidden surfaces in other cabinetry. Higher-quality particleboard is rated as 45-pound commercial grade; the rating refers to the pounds of pressure applied during production. Know the grade and thickness of particleboard used. Poor grades won't hold a screw, and thin sheets may warp.

■ **Medium-density fiberboard** is a high-quality substrate material made from finer fibers than particleboard. It offers a very smooth surface, and its edges can be shaped and painted. But it is not as strong as plywood and shouldn't be used as structural support.

■ **Plywood** is made by laminating thin layers of wood plies to each other, with the grain at right angles in alternate plies. Varying the direction of the plies gives plywood equal strength in all directions. Plywood comes in a variety of grades (A is for interior use) and thicknesses ($\frac{1}{4}$ to $1\frac{1}{8}$ inches) and is one of the best materials for structural support in cabinets.

MEASUREMENTS

A kitchen smaller than 150 square feet should have:
■ at least 13 feet of base cabinets
■ at least 12 feet of wall cabinets.
A larger kitchen should have:
■ at least 16 feet of base cabinets
■ at least 15½ feet of wall cabinets.

Cabinets

▲ *When you need new cabinets, consider the value of standard metal cabinetry. These tried-and-true components clean up easily, look great with appliances, and save you a bundle.*

Decorating Ideas

Avoid trendy colors that come and go for your permanent appliances, cabinetry, fixtures, and flooring. (Remember harvest gold and avocado green?) Stick with classic colors for these features. Apply the latest color trends with wallpaper and paint. When they go out of style, you can repaper and paint for a lot less than you can refinish cabinets or replace fixtures.

On the Surface

You'll be looking at the surface material you choose for cabinets every day, probably for years. Here are your choices:

■ **Wood cabinets** have universal appeal and are built to suit a wide range of styles. Although some softwood is used, most cabinets are made from hardwoods.

Before you select wood for your cabinets, consider whether you like the wood grain or just the wood color. Pigmented stains can reproduce the color of maple on a birch base, for example.

Also keep in mind that wood warps easily as its moisture content changes. That's why it's important that wood cabinets be finished on all sides before they leave the factory. Unfinished cabinetry brought into the home should be finished as soon as possible to prevent warping.

Solid wood is not the best material for large flat surfaces such as cabinet sides, bottoms, and shelves; plywood or particleboard works better in these areas. Veneers applied over plywood or particleboard are more stable than solid lumber in high humidity, and grains may match better.

■ **Plastic laminate** provides a smooth surface and a great variety of colors. It's fused to a core material such as particleboard. On cabinet doors, laminate should be applied both on the front and back to prevent warping.

There are high- and low-pressure laminates. High-pressure laminates give a better performance, but they are relatively expensive. Difficult to damage and to repair, these top-of-the-line laminates provide vertical surfaces with the same durability as countertops. Low-pressure laminates (also called melamine) work well for most vertical surfaces. They are less impact-resistant than high-pressure laminates, but using a high-quality substrate such as plywood or particleboard will help.

■ **Foils and vinyl films** step in for laminates on some cabinetry, but they do not offer the durability of laminates. Their main advantage is they cost less.

Finish Line

Wood stain, paint glaze, and paint are three popular finishes for wood cabinetry. The number of steps used to produce a silky smooth finish—wiping and sanding by hand—adds to the cost. It takes an expert touch with glazes to get even coverage over various types of wood.

■ **Wood stains and paint glazes** seep into the grain of the wood and, as a result, do not chip. (Nicks in the wood, however, will show.) Stains enhance wood tones; glazes add a variety of colors that play off the natural color of wood.

Stains and glazes are finished with top coats that provide durability and easy maintenance. For residential use, options include lacquer, catalyzed varnishes, and urethanes. Lacquer is a good finish that's easy to repair, but it is not as resistant to household cleansers as are the catalyzed varnishes and urethanes.

■ **Painted finishes** are susceptible to chipping and cracking, but many painted cabinets are finished with a baked-on, clear top coat that improves the durability of the finish.

Judging Quality

When you're shopping for quality, a close look will reveal much about the fit and finish of any cabinet. Look at several brands to get a feel for how well built they are. Cabinets fastened with metal clips or, even worse, staples are not good quality. Look for screws and dowels. Look for tight joints, evenly matched pieces of wood, doors that lie flat, and smooth top-coat finishes. If you see more flaws than you like, keep looking.

Quality Checks

■ Inspect the wood grain. On quality cabinets, the grain on the doors matches that on the frame.

■ Drawer construction indicates quality. If you pull a drawer out about an inch and let go, it should close itself. Look at the slides; a pair of metal slides is better than the nylon variety or a roller mechanism installed underneath the drawer. When the drawer is fully extended, there should be no side-to-side wavering.

■ Remove the drawer. Look for drawers assembled with screws and dowels rather than glue and staples. Another quality fastening method is dovetailing—an interlocking joint.

■ With the drawers out, peek inside the cabinet. Check for corner gussets or blocks at the stress points, such as corners just below the countertop. These features add strength and durability.

Cabinetry Costs

	Midline Stock	Semicustom	Top-of-the-line Semicustom	Carpenter-built Custom
Laminate	$95-$190	$130-$225	$270-$360	$260-$570
Veneer	$95-$190	N/A	N/A	$360-$690
Solid wood	$180-$270	$200-$360	$360-$420	$420-$750
Painted wood	$200-$360	$225-$270	$300-$400	$450-$930

Prices are per linear foot

Countertops

Choose a countertop material that stands the test of grime and use and looks great when the focus turns from meal preparation to entertaining.

Laminate

Laminate is the most popular countertop material, and it's easy to see why. It's inexpensive as well as low-maintenance and comes in a wide variety of colors, patterns, and textures.

Laminate is simply a $\frac{1}{16}$-inch-thick polymer bonded to $\frac{3}{4}$-inch plywood or particleboard with contact adhesive, but the look it provides doesn't have to be simple. Give a laminate countertop a square or rolled edge. Trim counter edges with wood or metal inlays to create a rich look.

Laminate resists grease and stains and cleans up with soap and water. However, laminate won't stand up to sharp knives or hot pans. Once damaged, laminate is difficult to repair.

Scratches and chips are harder to see with solid-color laminates, where color runs through the entire sheet. Solid-color products also can be routed to create graphic effects.

Do-it-yourselfers must use care when laying out plastic laminate—any seams should be at corners. Stresses at unbroken corners can lead to

cracking. Similarly, cutouts for sinks and cooktops should have rounded corners.

Prices start at about $15 per running foot installed. Solid colors and textured styles cost more than smooth patterns.

Ceramic Tile

Tile is durable and available in many colors, patterns, and sizes, from 1-inch squares to 6×8-inch rectangles. Customize your countertop and cut costs by using a combination of solid-color and patterned tiles.

Tile handles your hot pans without scorching and is moisture-resistant. Using a knife on tile is not suggested because it dulls the knife.

Generally, a quick wipe with a damp cloth is all it takes to clean tile. Grout joints are susceptible to stains, but in most cases stains can be removed with scouring powder and household bleach. Tiles with a high-gloss glaze tend to show wear more quickly.

On counters, tile is either set in a mortar bed underlayment or bonded to it. With practice, this can be a do-it-yourself undertaking. It must be installed carefully with tight grout joints. The grout should be treated and sealed to make it mildew-resistant.

The price of solid-color tiles starts at about $5 per square foot installed. Patterned tiles start about $2 apiece. Stain- and scratch-resistant finishes cost more.

Solid-Surface Material

Durability is the greatest selling point of solid-surface material. It's $\frac{1}{2}$ inch to $1\frac{1}{2}$ inches thick, solid color throughout, and self-supporting so it doesn't need underlayment. There are many colors and patterns to choose from, including styles that look like granite and other stones.

Since it's nonporous, solid-surface material resists mildew and stains. However, it can be damaged by sharp knives and hot pots. If the countertop is scorched or scratched, minor damage can be repaired with sandpaper.

Cost for solid-surface material starts at about $100 per running foot installed.

Butcher Block

A butcher-block countertop exudes the warmth of a natural material but requires special care. Think about installing butcher block in only one preparation counter where it will get a lot of use as a cutting and chopping board. It's not recommended for use around a sink because constant exposure to water causes staining and rotting.

Hardwoods such as red or white oak, hardrock maple, or beech are best for kitchen surfaces. The thickness of a wood countertop is usually between 1 inch and 1½ inches.

Unfinished wood requires periodic treatment with mineral oil. It also must be cleaned thoroughly after being used for food preparation. Any scratches can be smoothed out with sandpaper. If you have the wood finished, be careful. A finish that helps the wood stand up to moisture may not be safe for food preparation.

The price for butcher-block countertops starts at about $50 per running foot installed.

Stone

Granite and marble offer unmatched beauty and durability. It's their expense that may put them out of consideration.

The cost of stone starts at about $120 per running foot. Installation also is expensive because stone is heavy and hard to cut. Stone must by waxed and polished regularly to maintain its luster. Stone countertops start at ¾ inch thick, but because cut stone is brittle, you might need a thicker slab.

Granite is the most popular stone for countertops. It cleans easily and can handle water, hot pots, and sharp knives (although the knives will suffer). It also resists most stains and can be sealed to protect against all stains. Marble is more porous than granite and, therefore, more susceptible to staining. It must be resealed often.

Stainless Steel

This tough metal is impervious to stains and can withstand high temperatures. Stainless steel makes a good heat-proof surface, especially next to the cooktop. It will, however, show nicks and scratches and, if not supported properly by a solid, firm base, it can be dented.

Commercial cleaning products are available in both oil- and water-based formulas. Use only water-based cleaners where food is prepared. Wood cleaners, especially foaming types, work well on stainless steel. Avoid scouring powders.

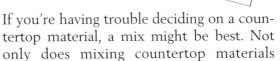

DESIGN DETAIL

If you're having trouble deciding on a countertop material, a mix might be best. Not only does mixing countertop materials give your kitchen a custom look, but it also can eliminate an inconvenient search for a cutting board or trivet for certain kitchen tasks.

For example, you could cover most of the work surface in an inexpensive laminate. A stone inset in the baking center will be perfect for rolling dough. A tile surface near the cooktop will handle hot-from-the-oven items. A butcher-block inset, *above*, will make a great chopping spot.

▲ *Black-and-white vinyl tiles act as a neutral backdrop and add fun to this country kitchen.*

▲ *Paint can give an old wood floor fresh character. This soft pine floor was first painted sunny yellow, then large white diamonds were added; finally, the colorful border was painted.*

Flooring

Don't overlook what's underfoot in your new kitchen. Colorful flooring makes a stylish statement but still must handle the everyday wear and tear of heavy traffic, bumps, and spills. Here's a look at three popular options.

Vinyl

Vinyl flooring is a natural for families with young children. A dropped glass has a good chance for survival, and messy spills clean up easily. The softness of the flooring cuts down on noise and is easy on the cook's feet and legs. Vinyl is also the least-expensive option, starting at about $4 per square foot installed.

The flooring is available in sheets or tiles. Sheet vinyls are more expensive than comparative grades of vinyl tiles, but they won't have the many seams tiles show. In most cases, sheet vinyls should be installed by professionals; tiles are an option for do-it-yourselfers.

Sheet vinyl is available in hundreds of colors and patterns and in widths from 6 to 12 feet. You can find vinyl that looks like marble, stone, ceramic tile, and wood.

Vinyl tiles are typically 12×12-inch squares, although some manufacturers offer tiles in smaller squares and in squares with diagonal corners and companion 1-inch filler squares. Options include solid and flecked colors, ceramic-tile patterns, brick, slate, and wood.

Vinyl planks, colored to look like wood, come in 3-inch-wide strips that can be installed much like genuine wood planks in random or herringbone patterns.

High-quality vinyl flooring can keep its good looks for decades. However, lower-quality vinyl flooring may show wear after five or six years.

Wood

Wood flooring complements any style, from country to contemporary, and blends nicely with most color schemes. New moisture-resistant finishes are increasing wood's popularity in the kitchen. Wood is also a forgiving surface for cooks who spend a lot of time on their feet. Prices start at about $7 per square foot installed.

Durable oak is the most popular wood for flooring. Pine is a favorite in country settings, too, because dents and nicks give it an authentic old-time look. Walnut, cherry, ash, and maple are among the other varieties you'll find.

Wood flooring falls into three categories: strip, plank, and parquet. Strip floors are made of narrow wood strips, typically 2¼ inches wide.

They're among the most economical wood floors to purchase.

Planks are wider than strips and come in many widths. You can buy same-width planks or vary the width of planks to add interest. Many have real or simulated wood plugs that add a colonial flair to the kitchen.

Parquet floors are made up of small wood pieces that are glued together in various patterns, including herringbone and block patterns. Parquet is the easiest type of wood flooring for do-it-yourself installation.

Stains for wood floors are available in a rainbow of colors. A polyurethane finish will protect the wood against spills, scratches, household chemicals, and wear.

Ceramic Tile

Easy maintenance and durability are the main assets of ceramic-tile flooring. Tile also presents unlimited decorating possibilities and unmatched style. However, the hard surface will be harder on feet and dropped dishes than vinyl or wood. Tile is also a noisy surface.

Ceramic tiles often are marketed in collections of mix-and-match colors, shapes, and sizes. To get ideas flowing, pick up some product booklets from dealers and manufacturers—they're brimming with ideas. You'll find 1×1- to 12×12-inch squares and geometric shapes in many sizes. Ceramic tiles come glazed or unglazed. Glazed tile is a good choice in the kitchen because liquids can't soak in. Some glazed surfaces may show wear in high-traffic areas.

Unglazed tile also can work in the kitchen but will require a bit more care. At least once a month, unglazed tiles should be cleaned with an oil-based detergent to protect pores.

The cost of ceramic tile starts at about $10 per square foot. The price will increase if the subfloor needs work to provide the rigid, strong underlayment needed for tile installation.

▲ *This ceramic tile floor is composed of 1×1-inch unglazed tiles laid in a pattern.*

THE RIGHT STUFF

Think beyond the look of your kitchen today when making decisions on flooring. When properly cared for, both wood and ceramic tile can look great for as long as you live in the house. Top-of-the-line vinyl flooring can last for 30 years or more.

Consider how long you want to live with the same king of flooring and pattern. If you like to change the look of your home periodically, you'll want to choose a neutral-color flooring that will go with a variety of decorating schemes. You can easily spice up the look of a plain floor with colorful rugs and runners.

If you want a flashier floor, you might want to choose an inexpensive vinyl that could be replaced without guilt after a few years. Vinyl and wood will also accept paint, so you could change the look without tearing out the flooring.

◄ *Capturing light is a prime goal for most kitchen remodelers. Large windows achieve that goal but may leave owners feeling that they are exposed to view. Divided windows like these minimize that effect.*

Windows

Selecting windows for the kitchen used to mean choosing one to go over the sink. Today there's a host of windows to choose from, including bays, corner windows, skylights, and sliders. Windows are placed high on the wall for privacy and even incorporated into the backsplash to let in as much light as possible.

In the energy-efficiency race, vinyl and wood windows rate ahead of aluminum units, but there's a cost for that advantage. Although prices vary according to availability and location, metal windows are usually the least expensive and wood the most expensive. Vinyl-frame windows require no painting and they'll never rot, but they won't look like wood.

Your choice of glass will also affect the cost, energy efficiency, and look of your windows. Insulated glass, particularly glass insulated with what is called low-emissivity glazing, not only reduces ultraviolet rays, but it also keeps warmth inside the room. Adding insulating argon gas between panes costs more but takes an additional step toward energy efficiency. When comparing windows, note the grades they get from the National Fenestration Rating Council. It's currently the best measuring and testing method to fairly compare the energy-efficient properties of different windows.

THE RIGHT STUFF

When selecting materials for your kitchen, take into account how well they absorb sounds. Wood absorbs more noise than vinyl, ceramic tile, or stone. Carpet absorbs sound better than any material. Fabrics on windows, upholstered furnishings, area rugs, even seat cushions absorb sound and can help reduce noise levels. Some out-of-sight materials, such as insulation in the tops of cabinetry, also help lower sound levels.

Smart Solutions

If you haven't shopped for windows in a while, the new technology may surprise you. Here are a few examples:

■ Special glazings are available that automatically adjust a window's transparency to compensate for changes in temperature or sun exposure. This means when the afternoon sun bears down on your kitchen, you won't overheat.

■ Marvin Windows offers Switchable Privacy Glass, a liquid crystal technology that can make a window frosted, or opaque. Flip a switch and an

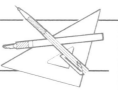

DESIGN DETAIL

The direction windows face will dictate the type of light that fills your kitchen. Southern and eastern windows, for example, will let in buttery warm sunlight. Eastern light is very bright, yet yields a more moderate temperature than a hotter southern exposure. Consider southern exposures for sunrooms, eastern ones for breakfast rooms. For entertaining, western light offers a warm and colorful backdrop. Indirect light from the north tends to be cooler, ideal for work areas.

▲ *This unusual combination of windows climbs the wall from the backsplash to above the cupboards.*

electrical current aligns the crystals for a clear view. This technology can help you dispense with window dressings, block the neighbor's view, or add a now-you-see-it, now-you-don't look between your kitchen and dining room.

■ Watch for window automation to lead the newest technological parade. No more running around to each pane; open, close, or lock windows with the push of a button. Hard-to-reach windows that previously stayed shut now can join the work force. Forget to close the window before you left the house? Don't worry, special sensors detect moisture and close automatically if it should rain.

To Do

Invest plenty of time into research and development of your project before plunging into demolition and reconstruction. Order product literature from manufacturers of materials and fixtures you'll need. Compile that literature in a project notebook, along with photographs from magazines and notes on your wants and needs. The goal is to arm yourself with as much information as you can in advance of committing yourself to action.

▲ *Here's a simple window covering idea: Attach decorative swag holders at both top corners of a window, then loosely drape fabric across the holders for a graceful touch.*

Choosing Fixtures And Appliances

PHASE 6: Don't choose appliances on their style alone; also check out their efficiency and durability.

The kitchen is indeed the home's most used room, and within those walls the fixtures and appliances do the lion's share of the work. They also represent anywhere from a couple to several thousand of your kitchen investment dollars. So, along with being stylish and functional, these components also must have the durability to earn their keep.

Be prepared to do some homework and ask sharp questions about each appliance you consider. The more you learn about what's available, the better your chances of purchasing components you'll be happy with for years.

➤ *Black and white ceramic tile teams up with stainless steel for commercial styling in this Chicago kitchen.*

◄ *Custom cabinets, granite countertops, hardwood flooring, and a side-by-side stainless-steel refrigerator complete the restaurant-style look.*

Buying Smart

Selecting the appropriate appliances and fixtures for your new kitchen is no easy task. Today's products are available in an ever-increasing array of types, sizes, and styles, with price tags as diverse as the features. Once your selections are made, you'll probably have to live with them for a decade or more—whether you're happy with your purchases or not. These shopping tips will help you make choices you can live with well into the future.

■ **Money matters.** First, establish a realistic budget. This step alone simplifies your purchase decisions and can help you sort out the necessary features from the luxury ones. A good approach to budget balancing is to splurge a little on one component and buy a lower-priced model of another component. You might, for example, want the biggest, best-made sink you can find but only need the smallest microwave for reheating coffee and leftovers.

■ **Check it out at the library first.** Study consumer publications that give brand-name ratings, available features, and prices. Before going shopping, take notes and narrow your choices to a few specific brands and models.

■ **Evaluate durability and serviceability.** The quality of the basic components of an appliance is more important than the number of novelty options. Such items as the power output of a microwave oven, the number of spraying arms in a dishwasher, and the storage capacity of a refrigerator/freezer are crucial to the appliance's value and dependability.

■ **Make sure it fits.** As you shop for appliances and fixtures, make sure you have a detailed list of the exact measurements you've allotted in your kitchen for each item. Remember, the product will be in your kitchen for many years, so you need to consider any potential changes in family size, lifestyle, and kitchen design when making capacity and size decisions.

■ **Shop for the best buys.** Don't just assume that an appliance warehouse has the best bargains. It's true that such companies buy directly from the manufacturers, but it is also common to find a group of smaller dealers who pool their resources to buy bigger volumes at discounted rates from the factory.

■ **Consider the value of a warranty along with the price.** Ask about the extent of the warranty. Which parts are covered? Does the warranty include labor? Will the warranty be honored by another dealer?

■ **Check on installation requirements.** Each appliance may have its own requirements. An icemaker on a refrigerator, for example, requires a water line. A downdraft fan on a cooktop eliminates the need for overhead ventilation, but the vent pipe needs outdoor access.

■ **Find out what is included in the price.** If an appliance requires professional installation, ask if that is included in the purchase price. If you decide to install the appliance yourself, be certain the installation charges aren't included in your purchase price.

Shopping Savvy

If you've always wanted a cooktop with ceramic-glass-covered radiant burners, don't settle for something less. Go over your list of must-haves and, using your budget as your guide, separate the essentials from the luxuries. If possible, keep a few luxury items on the list, so when the remodeling is done you'll be satisfied with the results instead of having regrets.

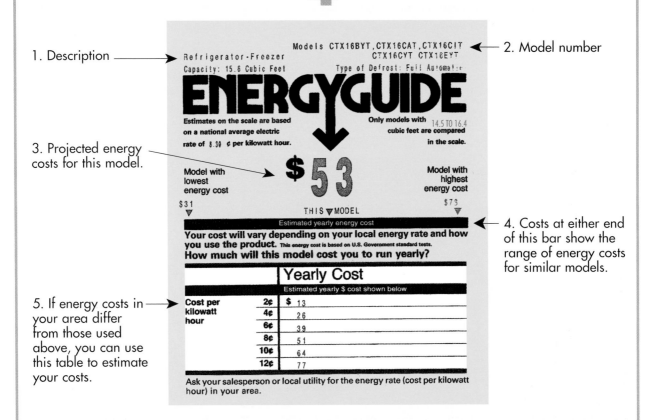

1. Description

2. Model number

3. Projected energy costs for this model.

4. Costs at either end of this bar show the range of energy costs for similar models.

5. If energy costs in your area differ from those used above, you can use this table to estimate your costs.

Models CTX16BYT, CTX16CAT, CTX16CIT CTX16CYT CTX16EYT

Refrigerator-Freezer
Capacity: 15.6 Cubic Feet

Type of Defrost: Full Automatic

ENERGYGUIDE

Estimates on the scale are based on a national average electric rate of 8.30 ¢ per kilowatt hour.

Only models with 14.5 TO 16.4 cubic feet are compared in the scale.

$53

Model with lowest energy cost

$31

THIS ▼ MODEL

Model with highest energy cost

$73

Estimated yearly energy cost

Your cost will vary depending on your local energy rate and how you use the product. This energy cost is based on U.S. Government standard tests.

How much will this model cost you to run yearly?

Yearly Cost
Estimated yearly $ cost shown below

Cost per kilowatt hour		
2¢	$	13
4¢		26
6¢		39
8¢		51
10¢		64
12¢		77

Ask your salesperson or local utility for the energy rate (cost per kilowatt hour) in your area.

Every appliance may have a price tag, but the real cost isn't determined until you take it home, plug it in, and live with it for a year.

To help you figure out the long-term expense of owning your appliance, the government requires manufacturers to label each item with an energy guide. This bright yellow tag helps consumers estimate the cost of running the appliance for one year.

Here is a closer look at one tag, showing how it can help you plan your budget.

1. This part describes the major appliance so you can compare accurately with others.

2. This section provides specific company and model information.

3. The utility rate used to average the cost may not be the same as yours, so check your utility bills and adjust costs accordingly for a more accurate estimate of your true cost.

4. This bar on the label does not tell you which models are the most and least energy efficient, but it does provide you with the top and bottom of the range, so you can compare the appliance's efficiency with that of appliances at the extremes.

5. This section lets you chart local utility rates to find your adjusted annual cost.

More efficient appliances usually cost the most, but it won't take long for accumulated energy-cost savings to pay for the difference between a low-priced and a high-priced appliance; plus, you'll continue to save year after year so a more expensive but more energy-efficient appliance will be less costly the longer you own it.

Sinks and Faucets

Most of your kitchen chores involve the sink, so choose a bowl and faucet that will be versatile as well as durable.

Material Choices

■ **Stainless steel** is the most popular sink material. It's the least expensive choice, with a basic double bowl starting at about $150. Stainless steel is also durable and lightweight, making it easy to install.

Consider the quality of the metal. A sink made of mirror-finish, 22-gauge stainless steel will show scratches and water spots and be susceptible to denting. A better choice is a 19-gauge nickel-and-stainless-steel sink with a brushed finish. The stronger steel resists denting, the nickel content wards off water spots, and the brushed finish hides scratches. With the increased quality comes increased cost.

Another option you may want for aesthetics is a stainless-steel sink coated with enamel. Though expensive, this type of sink still is susceptible to chipping and staining.

■ **Enameled cast iron** is a better choice for a sink with a color coating. It's resistant to chipping and will keep its shine even after years of use. Whereas stainless steel tends to blend into the background in the kitchen, a bright-colored sink commands attention. Some popular choices

Home Safety

Don't store potentially dangerous household chemicals and cleaning agents under the sink. Common sense says that poisons and caustic substances should be kept out of a child's reach, so plan a high storage area in the wall cabinet above the refrigerator or on the upper shelves of a pantry cabinet.

include shiny black, cherry red, bright blue, and forest green. One drawback is that the weight of a cast-iron sink can make installation more difficult. The cost of a basic cast-iron sink is about $200 without installation.

■ **Vitreous china, quartz composite, and solid-surface material** are a few of the more expensive choices. Vitreous china is easy to clean but can chip. Quartz composite resists scratches and stains and looks great with a stone countertop. Solid-surface material offers solid colors as well as stone look-alikes. The major advantage to solid-surface material is that the sink and countertop can be all one piece for easy cleaning.

Shapes and Features

Sinks come in several configurations. You can buy a single-bowl (ideal for soaking big pots and pans); a double-bowl (good for handling food preparation and dish-soaking simultaneously); a triple-bowl (the center-well disposer corrals scraps while you prepare food or wash dishes in the main bowls); or an L-shaped corner sink in either a double- or triple-bowl configuration (good for small kitchens with limited counter space). For each of these you can buy fitted cutting boards to place over the basins, thus extending counter space. Still another useful feature to look for is an extra-deep basin. Some reach down to 14 inches, which can be useful for handling tall pots and loading in lots of dishes and cookware.

In terms of installation, most sinks are the self-rimming type and have a perimeter lip that sits on and seals to the counter with a bead of caulk. These are the easiest to install, especially when it comes to handling heavy cast iron. Another style is the under-mount sink, so called for the way it fastens under the counter cutout. This type pairs well with solid counter materials (stone and solid-surface material) and leaves a convenient flush surface that's easy to clean. There is, however, a seam between the counter and the sink that has to be kept clean.

Faucets

Kitchen faucets don't just deliver water anymore; they scrub, spray, even conserve water and control its temperature. The cost of faucets reflects their varied functions, from $40 for a basic chrome model to more than $800 for a faucet that turns on when a hand or dish breaks an infrared sensor.

Brushed and polished chrome, which once dominated faucet finishes, remain popular. Other choices gaining attention include powder-coat epoxy in vibrant colors and polished brass.

Leaky faucets are becoming a thing of the past. Some faucets are being made without washers; others replace the rubber rings with plastic or ceramic disks.

Special faucet features and accessories can make your work in the kitchen easier. Some faucets come with scraper/spray and brush/spray combinations for tough cleaning jobs. Others contain pullout wands that change from stream to spray at the push of a button. Pullout spray arms and riser faucets also adjust to make room for large pots or buckets.

Temperature controls also are an asset. Antiscald faucets allow you to set the maximum water temperature to protect children. Instant hot- or chilled-water dispensers keep water on tap for coffee, soups, and powdered drink mixes.

▲ *Interchangeable pullout spouts on this curved white faucet help it perform a variety of cleaning duties. Its extra height makes room for large pots. The single-handle water control makes it easier to adjust the water temperature with one hand.*

DESIGN DETAIL

When shopping for the perfect sink for your new kitchen, think twice. With cooking becoming more of a family affair, two sinks may be better than one.

With a main sink in the countertop and a small bar-type sink in the island, two cooks can work together without getting in each other's way. If you decide to put a sink in the island, the best location is at one end near the refrigerator. Putting the sink in the middle of the island will cut down on the amount of continuous work surface you have.

Dishwashers, Disposers, and Compactors

Dishwashers and garbage disposers are standard equipment in modern kitchens. Even the trash compactor is considered a necessity by some homeowners. Here's what to look for when you're shopping.

Dishwashers

Dishwasher options run from basic models with stationary racks, one wash arm, and two cycles to top-of-the-line units with adjustable racks, four wash arms, six cycles, and other attractive features. Maytag has introduced a model that selects the wash cycle for you based on the amount of food soil in the water, how long it's been since the last wash, and even how many times the door has opened since the last wash.

You can purchase a basic dishwasher for about $250. Of course, price rises with options, so consider your needs carefully. For instance, if you only use your good china and crystal twice a year, you probably don't need a special china-and-crystal cycle on your new dishwasher.

Other special features on high-quality models include a built-in disposer, an interior light, a delayed-start option so the dishwasher can do its work when electricity rates are lower, and its own internal water heater. The boost provided by the dishwasher's water heater gets water temperature to the 140 degrees necessary to cut grease. It also allows you to set your household water heater at a lower temperature, which not only saves you money, but also lets you wash dishes and not worry about taking a cold shower.

▲ Linger over dessert—not dishes—with the delayed-start Excellence dishwasher (about $1,000). It holds 14 place settings and features short wash cycles. From ASKO, Inc.

▲ Maytag's new IntelliSense dishwasher uses sensors to determine the optimal wash and rinse cycles.

Washing a full load of dishes by hand can take up to 16 gallons of water, and older dishwashers don't work much more efficiently than that. But today's units have cut that amount of water consumption by half or even more.

Dishwashers are also doing their jobs more quickly (although it still takes most machines more than an hour to get through a load) and more quietly. Now that kitchens often share space with family rooms, noise level should be considered. No one wants to carry on a conversation while competing with a dishwasher.

The key to cutting noise is choosing a model that is well-insulated. You can do more to muffle the dishwasher by placing it in or behind an island that separates the kitchen from the family room. By the time the sound makes its way around the obstacle, it won't be as loud.

Garbage Disposers

If you're not going to compost food wastes, a garbage waste disposer is an effective way to get rid of them down the drain, provided you have a sewer connection and not a septic system.

Batch-feed disposers grind from 1 to 2 quarts of waste at a time and are controlled by a built-in switch activated by replacing the drain lid. A continuous-feed disposer usually is controlled by a wall switch and lets you continuously feed waste into the disposer as it runs. With either type, it's important to run a constant flow of cold water when grinding to move the waste through the drain line.

When you shop for a garbage disposer, look for a sturdy motor, ½ horsepower or greater; an overload protector; automatic reversing of the blades to help free jams; and plenty of noise insulation. Expect to pay $45 to $190 for a garbage disposer, plus installation.

Trash Compactors

When they first appeared, trash compactors were an answer to the ever-increasing volume of household garbage. Now, with mandatory recycling taking bottles, cans, plastics, and all sorts of paper out of the mix, there may be less of a need to compress what's left. Most of us can't forgo

▲ KitchenAid's slim trash compactor slips neatly between the cabinetry.

▲ This sample of garbage disposers shows the range of sizes offered in the marketplace today.

recycling, so unless your household generates a large volume of nonrecyclable trash, think long and hard about getting a compactor. If you decide you want one, consider the following features when you go shopping.
- a removable rammer to simplify cleanup
- a key-activated on/off switch for added safety
- a toe-touch door latch for easy opening
- a built-in air filter or deodorizer
- trim kits for mounting a cabinet door panel.

Refrigerators

▲ *This new side-by-side 21-cubic-foot refrigerator from Whirlpool has a shallow depth (24 inches) so it doesn't stick out beyond cabinets as most side-by-sides do. It comes with a trim kit so you can add your own panels to match your cabinets, giving a custom look.*

There are three types of refrigerators to consider.

■ **A top-mount refrigerator** consists of a separate freezer compartment over the main food storage space. It's the most efficient refrigerator to operate and puts freezer items at a convenient height.

■ **In a bottom-mount model,** the freezer compartment is near the floor. This setup puts the most frequently used refrigerator space at a more accessible height. The freezer is like a drawer, which is especially handy for a seated cook.

■ **With the refrigerator and freezer placed side by side,** less space is needed for opening doors. That makes this design a good fit for narrow galley kitchens. Although a side-by-side freezer compartment offers more cubic feet of storage at more convenient levels, the unit's shelves and door are sometimes too small to hold larger containers and bulky frozen items.

Side-by-side models (starting at about $900) are more expensive than top- or bottom-mount units, which start at about $600.

When pricing refrigerators, it's important to consider operating costs, too. Read the yellow energy guide label on models you are considering (see page 77).

Also consider options that will make the refrigerator fit your family, including:

■ Adjustable deep door bins that can hold 1- or 2-liter containers and gallon milk jugs.

■ Sliding shelves that make cleaning easy and bring items into better view. The shelves adjust so you can store tall items without having to completely rearrange the refrigerator.

■ Refreshment centers that let you store and serve frequently used snacks and beverages without opening the main door.

■ A flip-down door/serving tray for access to frequently used items.

■ Separate temperature and humidity controls for meat, fruit, and vegetable compartments.

■ Sealed storage dishes that fit just below the shelf offer convenient storage for leftovers. The dishes can go from the refrigerator to the microwave oven to the dishwasher.

■ An automatic icemaker ends the hassle of refilling cube trays and running out of ice. Getting water to it requires a small, ¼-inch water line that taps into the nearest cold-water line, perhaps by the sink or dishwasher or in the basement through a hole drilled in the floor.

■ Cold-water, beverage, and ice-cube dispensers on the outside of the refrigerator door are not only convenient, they also save energy: You don't waste cooled air by opening the door so often.

Balance the cost of any extras against how often you use them. Don't forget less flashy considerations such as quality construction, quiet operation, and automatic defrost.

Sizing Up Your Needs

Cubic feet can be a confusing concept when trying to figure out cold-storage needs. As a rule, start with 12 cubic feet of total refrigerator/freezer space for the first two family members. Add 2 cubic feet for each additional person.

Beyond these guidelines, consider your lifestyle: how often you eat at home, how often you shop for fresh foods, how far you are from a grocery store, and how often you entertain. Don't pay to cool more space than you'll use, but don't scrimp either. An over-filled unit will have limited air circulation and cost more to operate.

Cooking Equipment

With increasing types of ranges, cooktops, and ovens, you now have more cooking options than ever. Before you start shopping, assess what you like and dislike about your present cooking equipment, then make a near-future projection of your family's cooking needs. If your family is growing, or if your next kitchen is planned for two cooks instead of one, your equipment needs may change.

Next evaluate the space limitations in your kitchen. It may be nice, for example, to have a separate cooktop and wall oven instead of a range, but not if it steals from valuable, limited counter or storage space.

Ranges

With burners on top and an oven below, the range is the most common piece of cooking equipment. There are four variations.

■ **A freestanding range** rests on the floor as a self-contained unit and is normally 30 inches wide. There are 24- and 36-inch-wide models available, with the latter usually having a fifth burner and an extra-wide oven.

■ **A hi-low range** not only has an oven and burners, but it also has a built-in microwave oven perched at about eye level.

continued

Cook Like a Pro

If you want a restaurant-style range or refrigerator for your kitchen, many of today's commercial-appliance manufacturers make an intermediate (often called "professional") line designed for home use. Like commercial appliances, they're built to last 30 years or more.

Before buying one for your home, make sure the size, appearance, and function fit your decorating tastes. Stainless steel doesn't blend with every color scheme, although it will reflect colorful accents, and the size of these appliances may overpower your kitchen. You must also determine if your budget can accommodate the substantial cost.

Professional gas ranges are equipped with larger ovens and usually have six or more burners. Flames can be set from an ultra-low 950 Btus (a unit of measuring heat energy) to more than 15,000 Btus. Typical residential ranges produce 9,000 to 11,000 Btus of heat. Many offer grills, griddles, and wok rings. Cooktops cost from $1,600 to $2,100. Ranges are $2,000 to more than $7,500.

Professional refrigerators and freezers pack more storage room and do an excellent job of maintaining proper temperature. They have the same stainless-steel look as commercial refrigerators. They generally run quietly and come with popular features, such as icemakers, automatic defrost, and adjustable storage bins. Costs range from $1,300 to $1,800.

Cooking Equipment

■ **A slide-in range** is simply a freestanding range without side panels. It fits in a 30-inch opening between base cabinets; if one side will be exposed, you can install a side panel for a more finished look.

■ **A drop-in range** is much like a slide-in except in the way it's installed. It must be permanently fastened to the base cabinets and usually rests on a built-up wood base. Without a bottom drawer, broilers in drop-in units are inside the oven. Drop-in and some slide-in units are well-suited for installation in an island or peninsula because there is no transom to interrupt the surface.

▲ *This slim-line sealed gas, glass cooktop from Creda easily fits over drawer space or over an electric oven.*

Cooktops

Traditional gas and electric-coil cooktops continue to be the most common choices for surface cooking. Gas burners will heat up and cool off more quickly than electric elements, and cooks can easily see and adjust the height of the flame to suit their needs. Some homeowners opt for electric to avoid the open flame and gas fumes. Other options are magnetic induction and halogen heating.

If no single cooktop seems to fit all your needs, consider a modular unit—a cooktop with interchangeable components. These include electric coils, sealed gas burners, a grill, a wok, a deep fryer, a griddle, or even a downdraft ventilator cartridge.

Costs range from less than $200 for a basic electric cooktop to more than $3,000 for a magnetic-induction unit.

Sealed gas burners

A significant improvement on the basic flame, sealed gas burners extend the cooking surface snugly around the heating element so spills stay on the surface where they are easy to clean. Some models have removable porcelain burner caps, which add to the unified styling.

Most cooktops with sealed gas burners are equipped with an energy-saving electronic ignition. To light the burner, turn the knob to the lighting position, and the burner will light in three seconds or less. Some models also will automatically relight the burner should the flame go out during cooking.

▲ *The new 30-inch freestanding range from Thermador installs into existing cabinetry cutouts.*

▲ *This new ceramic-glass electric cooktop from Dacor features an innovative command center controlled by the touch of a finger.*

Solid-disk elements

Similar to cooktops with sealed gas burners, these electric cooktops are also easy to clean. Instead of coils, these Eurostyle cooktops have a solid cast-iron cooking surface that contains electrical wires below. Slower to heat and cool than traditional coils, these burners are coated with a noncorrosive surface, grooved for traction, and surrounded by a stainless-steel spill ring.

Some solid-disk cooktops have sensors that automatically lower the temperature before food boils over. If you're not ready to give up the cooktop you have, you can replace standard electric coils with solid disks for about $250.

Ceramic glass

Ceramic-glass cooktops feature special electric coils or halogen elements under a see-through ceramic-glass cover. The smooth cooktop is attractive and easy to clean.

Ceramic glass is shock- and scratch-resistant and withstands temperatures of more than 1,300

▲ *This barbecue grill cooktop manufactured by Russell Range has a polished brass front.*

degrees. Coils glow red when the burner is on, and the glass will stay hot for a while after the burner is off. You may want to shut the burner off early and finish cooking on retained heat to help ease that problem.

The cooktops often will combine heat options. You may have three high-speed radiant electric elements and one halogen burner. The mix helps cut costs since halogen is expensive.

Halogen heat works in a fashion similar to an incandescent lightbulb. With a halogen bulb, 10 percent of the energy given off is light; the rest is heat. Halogen burners will heat faster than electric ones, providing more flexibility for the cook. Cookware with thick, flat bottoms heats most efficiently on smooth-top cooktops.

Magnetic induction

Magnetic-induction cooktops are sometimes called cool-tops because the pan—not the surface—cooks the food. An electromagnetic field generates the heat.

Magnetic-induction cooktops are smooth like ceramic glass, making them easy to clean. In fact, you can get burners that look like ceramic tiles so it's hard to tell at a glance where countertop ends and cooktop begins.

continued

THE RIGHT STUFF

Purchasing a range that includes the cooktop and the oven in one unit is cheaper than buying a separate wall oven and cooktop. Having just one appliance also eliminates the need for running electric or gas lines to the separate units.

If your kitchen is small, a range can be a big space-saver. However, if you use your oven frequently, a range means a lot of bending, and anyone working at the cooktop will be in your way.

Whether you choose a range or a wall oven, you'll probably want a self-cleaning one. That feature will add $100 or more to the cost of the machine.

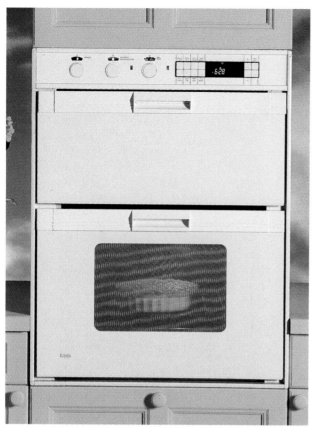

▲ *This double oven from Creda features a convection oven on top with a conventional oven on the bottom. Also fitted in the top oven is an integral broiler and spit/rotisserie.*

Ovens

The way ovens are used in most kitchens today reflects families' busy lifestyles. Also, the conventional oven is increasingly being installed in pairs for two cooks. The choices you make for your own kitchen will depend on the way you cook.

Conventional

A conventional oven is the type people are most familiar with. Also referred to as radiant-heat or thermal-heat ovens, conventional units consist of two heating elements: one for baking and roasting, and one for broiling.

With heat radiating up and pushing cold air down, there is a potential for uneven heating. For instance, if you fill both racks of a conventional oven with sheets of cookies, those on the bottom will burn before the ones on top are done. In newer conventional ovens, the top element comes on during baking for more even browning. Prices for conventional wall ovens, either electric or gas, start at around $400.

Convection

Convection ovens circulate heated air for faster, even cooking. A fan installed in the back wall of the oven blows the hot air around. This even heat distribution enables you to use more of the oven space. For example, you could stack two or three cookie sheets in the oven without fear of burning those on the bottom rack.

Convection ovens warm up faster to cut preheating time. They also will cut down on cooking time for some dishes. The drawback is that forced air may dry out some foods, and you may have to cover some items to prevent overbrowning.

Also consider the noise of the fan when deciding between conventional and convection ovens. Check with the manufacturer on steps taken to muffle the sound.

Many ovens offer both convection and conventional heat. Prices for combination wall ovens begin at about $1,000.

Microwave

The convenience of the microwave oven has made it an indispensable tool in the kitchen. In fact, some families are requesting two microwaves: one near the cooktop to assist in meal preparation (warming rolls, steaming vegetables, melting butter) and one near the refrigerator to serve as a snack center (reheating leftovers, making popcorn, warming hot chocolate). The falling price of the microwave makes it easier to own a pair. A midsize microwave that offers some preprogrammed selections sells for about $200 today. In the early 1980s, a comparable unit sold for as much as $700.

Despite its popularity and price, the microwave is not without drawbacks. For example, meat won't come out the way you're used to since most microwaves don't have browning capabilities (although some top-of-the-line models have the capacity to brown foods near the end of a cooking cycle).

Advances in heat distribution are starting to address the problem of having to turn dishes in microwaves for more even cooking. Turntables are another answer. Some microwaves will interrupt a cooking mode and flash a signal to turn the food before the cycle continues.

On the plus side, the microwave won't heat up the kitchen the way a full-size oven will, and preprogrammed control settings such as "popcorn," "defrost by weight," and "automatic reheat" take the guesswork out of some common applications you may want to use.

Combination

Many appliance manufacturers offer ovens with combination heating systems: convection and microwave heat, convection and conventional heat, or microwave and conventional heat. You can find double wall ovens that make use of all three heat sources. For example, a microwave could be placed over a convection/conventional oven combination to fill all cooking needs.

If space is hard to come by in your kitchen, these combination ovens may be just what you need. Buying a combination oven, however, is just as expensive as buying separate ovens; in some instances, it may cost more. And microwaving a cup of coffee in a large wall oven takes longer than in a small microwave, since the waves must travel farther.

Hoods and Vents

Shopping for a ventilation system may not be as glamorous as considering new cooktops, but it's just as important. Surface cooking releases heat, steam, grease, and odors that you don't want floating around your new kitchen. Your choices in ventilation are updraft and downdraft systems, and ducted and ductless systems.

▲ *The unobtrusive updraft ventilator over this cooktop is ducted through top cupboards and out the exterior wall.*

An updraft system consists of a hood that pulls air up through a filter and along ductwork to the outside. Downdraft systems, which can fit flush on the cooktop or rise 6 inches or so at the back, draw air down and out through ductwork under the floor. If your cooktop is on an island, a downdraft system may be more desirable. However, if your home doesn't have a basement for installing ductwork, you'll probably need an updraft system.

If you have a duct system, above all, be sure the ventilator is ducted outside. Ductless (or recirculating) range hoods filter soot and some odors, but most pollutants are recirculated right back into the room. Using one of these can be like cooking on a campfire in your kitchen. Never use a ductless hood with a gas range.

continued

Cooking Equipment

Burns and scalds happen all too frequently. In a typical accident, someone loses control of a pot trying to remove it from the cooking surface, and the contents spill and scald the cook. Accessible set-down spaces next to the cooking surface minimize burn risk because the pot can be slid off the burner rather than lifted. Fifteen to 18 inches on either side of a surface cooking unit is recommended. This space also provides room for swiveling pot handles out of the traffic flow and out of the reach of children.

Range-top fires are rare, but they do happen. Burning grease or fat cannot be extinguished with water, so mount a chemical-compound fire extinguisher near the cooking area where you can reach it in a hurry.

Ducted range hoods use fans or blowers. Propeller-style fans twist air up the exhaust duct, causing the air to drag against its sides and reducing the exhaust output. More efficient blowers have squirrel-cage mechanisms that suck air without causing as much turbulence and reducing the air's drag against the side of the duct.

To choose a hood, measure the cooking surface to make sure the hood will cover all the burners. At a store, watch hoods in action. Look for a design that pulls rising cooking vapors and contains them until the blower can carry them outside. Be sure the hood can be installed no higher than 30 inches above the cooking surface.

Choose a system with a rating of at least 150 cubic feet per minute. Restaurant-style ranges or hoods longer than 48 inches wide may need extra blowers. Other factors being equal, check the system's sone (sound) ratings. The lower the rating, the quieter the ventilator.

Lighting

Lighting needs to be good and bright in a kitchen so you can see what you're doing. Develop your lighting plan based on three approaches: general or ambient lighting, task lighting, and accent lighting (see drawing *facing page*).

General or Ambient Lighting

A basic form of lighting that replaces sunlight, ambient light casts a comfortable level of brightness throughout a room. It need not come from one source. In fact, a room is usually more pleasing when overall lighting comes from a blend of sources. In a medium-size kitchen (smaller than 120 square feet), you could center one ceiling-mounted fixture (two or more for larger kitchens) and add recessed spotlights around the room's perimeter.

Task Lighting

Focusing on a specific spot (such as the chopping center, baking counter, or cleanup area), task lighting should be bright enough to prevent eyestrain. Take care that the light shines on the work surface and isn't blocked by the worker.

Accent Lighting

This spotlights the best features of your room, such as artwork or architectural elements, taking attention away from a stack of dirty utensils and dishes. Track, recessed, or wall-mounted fixtures provide useful accent lights.

To find out more about your options, visit a lighting supply store. Expect to be dazzled, if not overwhelmed, by the myriad possibilities. Bring in your kitchen plans for expert advice on what fixtures to get and where they should go.

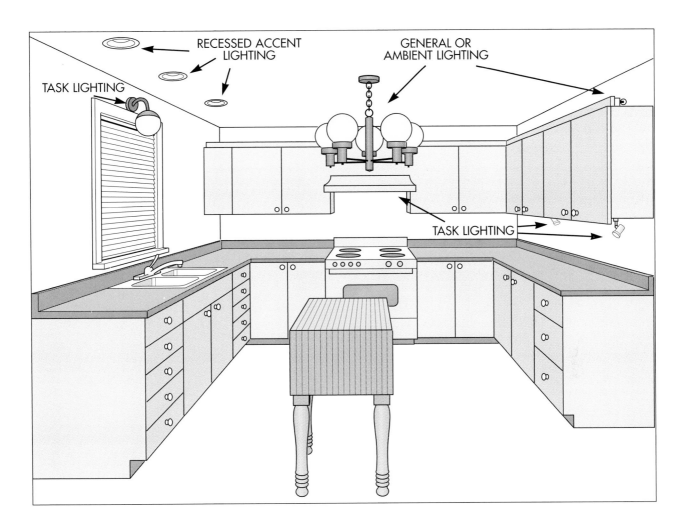

Types of Lightbulbs

Each type of lightbulb has advantages and disadvantages. Here's a rundown:

■ **Incandescent bulbs.** Still the most commonly used light source, incandescent bulbs cost the least up front and cast a warm, pleasant light. However, they produce a lot of heat.

■ **Fluorescent bulbs.** Although a fluorescent lamp can cost as much as 12 times more than a standard incandescent bulb, it uses only one-third the electricity and costs less over time. Fluorescent lamps last longer in fixtures that aren't turned on and off frequently. For kitchens, specify color-corrected, or warm white, tubes.

■ **Tungsten-halogen lights.** A low-voltage type of incandescent bulb, tungsten (or halogen) light provides an intense beam ideal for accenting. While incandescents grow dim with age, halogen

lamps produce a consistently bright, white light as long as the bulb lasts, which is often four times longer than regular incandescents. These lamps also use less electricity.

DESIGN DETAIL

These days designers are using a lot of combination lighting in kitchen projects. Ceiling lights, for example, are recessed cans with halogen bulbs that give off a bright white, energy-efficient light. Because the light is so bright, fewer cans can be used. Low-voltage halogens make good under-cabinet lighting. If you want softer light, use halogen bulbs in the ceiling and low-voltage incandescents installed under cabinetry.

Developing Your Design

PHASE 7: It's time to pull all your ideas together into a written plan. Here's how.

At this point you should have your remodeling strategy firmly in mind. The next step is drawing a detailed plan, accurate to a small fraction of an inch—technically, you'll be designing and building with tolerances of $1/16$ to $1/8$ inch.

Along with a basic strategy, you should have a pretty good idea what kind of layout you want (U-shaped, galley, etc.), the shape of the work triangle, and how the activity areas will be arranged. It's also helpful to have a sense of the materials you'll be using and the overall style you want to create.

This also is the time to decide on your cabinet strategy. Are you going to build the cabinets yourself, have them made by a local shop, or buy stock cabinets or ready-to-assemble units?

If some of these areas need more detailed decisions made about them, do it now. This phase depends upon knowing what you want. There will indeed be discovery and change as you create your layout, but try to answer as many questions as possible now so you won't be making hasty design decisions during the building phase.

➤ *Before remodeling, constant traffic through this kitchen disrupted cooking tasks. Now, a family-efficient, L-shaped food center opens to a sunny, casual dining nook. As in any remodeling, details make the difference: Notice the electrical outlet placed conveniently in the side of the island, for example.*

Architect: Dale Mulfinger

Sharpen Your Pencils

There's no mystery about the steps needed to reach your final plan. First, the space you're remodeling has to be carefully measured then drawn to scale, both in a plan view (looking down from directly overhead) and in elevation form (looking directly at each wall). For clarity on your floor plan, use dotted lines to show wall cabinets and solid lines to show base units. Use this carefully measured floor plan to play around with the space, drawing rough sketches until you have a design you like.

Then use the templates provided in this chapter to get a basic layout. Place the sink and appliances first, then the cabinets. When you're satisfied with the plan, draw it up in final form, complete with interior elevations, labeling important details. With your plan thus finalized, concentrate on completing a detailed materials list that will give you a good estimate of what the work will cost (see page 110).

Together, these items (the final plan elevations and materials list) are the culmination of the design phase. Take them to a design professional, if you like, who will double-check your work and offer suggestions for improvement. Or, if you have confidence in the design, give it directly to your builder and cabinetmaker.

Before construction begins, you're required by law to submit plans for approval to the local building code enforcement office. The code official will notify you if the design is in violation of code. Door widths, ceiling heights, electrical outlets, and plumbing fixtures are where most of the spacing requirements will be scrutinized.

So, sharpen your pencils. Pick up your tape measure. Here comes your kitchen.

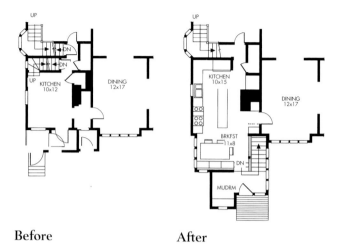

Before   After

How This Plan Works

Throughout this chapter we'll be using the kitchen pictured on pages 90–91 and 93 as a model of good design. We chose this particular kitchen because it's an excellent example of a popular remodeling effort—uncramping a small kitchen in an older house and building a small addition for a back entrance and eating area. Not only is the kitchen work area artfully arranged, but when combined with the sunny addition, the whole keeping room becomes the warm, lively heart of the home.

This remodeling occurred in a 1920s Craftsman-style home in Minneapolis. Typical of such houses, the original kitchen was dark, cramped, and constantly disrupted by traffic. A 140-square-foot addition proved to be the perfect solution. The result is astounding—a spacious, traditionally styled kitchen with enough room for serious cooking as well as casual family eating, informal entertaining, and a spot for after-school homework.

By pushing out the rear of the house 11 feet, architect Dale Mulfinger gained the square footage he needed to shove the basement stairs and pantry out of the main traffic flow and build a well-planned mudroom and sunny dining area. From the eating area, surrounded by windows, you can step out to the mudroom and backyard or down the handcrafted stairway to the laundry.

▲ *This modern-day keeping room, a recent addition, is detailed to match the Craftsman-style original architecture: divided-light windows, wide moldings, a transom over the back door, hardwood flooring, and oak structural columns, balusters, and newel post.*

MEASUREMENTS

In designing your kitchen, exercise creativity by all means, but keep in mind these standard dimensions for efficiency and lower cost:

■ Factory-built base cabinets are normally made in 3-inch increments from 12 to 48 inches wide and 24 inches deep (front to back). The total height is usually 34½ inches, including a toe-kick height at the bottom of the base cabinets of 4 inches.

■ Wall cabinets range from 12 to 48 inches wide and 12 to 13 inches deep.

■ Appliances placed opposite one another require 5 to 6 feet of clearance so that doors can open at the same time without interfering with each other.

■ Counter surfaces are usually 36 inches high. Allow 15 to 18 inches clearance between a countertop and the underside of the wall cabinet above it for small appliances such as a blender, mixer, or coffeemaker.

■ For standard-depth cabinets over a sink, allow at least 30 inches above the sink rim.

■ Height to the bottom of upper cabinets should be 4 feet, 6 inches from the floor or 1½ feet from the countertop.

Measuring Up

Remodeling your kitchen successfully starts with a clear picture of the space you have to work with. Forget for the moment existing cabinets, counters, appliances, and other components. Imagine an empty room—nothing except walls, floor, and ceiling.

This stage is called "measuring up" because that's exactly what's involved: taking careful measurements and drawing up an accurate, scaled floor plan. If you are lucky enough to have the original blueprints of your house, you've got a head start on this, but you'll still have to check them against the room's actual dimensions to be certain the house was built as planned. Measuring up also can reveal flaws—walls not plumb, corners not square, floors not level—that can affect both final cabinet dimensions and how the cabinets are installed.

The first step in this phase is collecting measurements. To avoid errors, don't measure with a yardstick or a cloth tape. Use only a steel tape, preferably up to 25 feet long. Record measurements in both feet and inches; because cabinets and appliances are measured in inches, this will save you from converting later.

Recording the Room

1. Carefully measure the perimeter dimensions of the room and draw an outline of it on ¼-inch graph paper at a scale of ¼ inch per foot (see page 109). Use a ruler to keep lines straight and a triangle to keep lines perpendicular.

2. Measure and label more detailed dimensions. Start in a corner and work your way around the room in one direction. Place the rule against the wall at a height of 36 inches and measure from the corner to the trim edge of the nearest doorway or window. Note this measurement to the nearest ¹/₁₆ inch. Also measure and note the width of the trim.

3. Measure and note the location and width of each doorway and window (the space between the inside edges of the trim). Also note the hing-

ing and swing of each door, and where it extends. Use dotted lines to outline the entire area through which doors will swing.

4. Measure from the floor to the bottom edge of the trim under the windowsill (called the window stool). For any window that will be over a counter, this measurement determines the height of the backsplash. It's also possible to cut down the width of the stool or eliminate it and have the backsplash go right up under the sill.

5. Measure the height of the room from floor to ceiling. Take this measurement in all corners and at midpoints in each wall, checking to see if the floor is level. Record any discrepancies.

6. With a partner, measure from a couple of points along a wall to the same points on the opposite wall (again, 36 inches up from the floor) to see if either wall is bowed in or out. If possible, take diagonal, corner-to-corner measurements to see if the room is square. If in a rectangular or square room the two diagonals aren't equal, you can find out the degree of error in each corner by using the 3-4-5 right-triangle method, shown *below*. Measure 3 feet out from the corner on one wall and 4 feet out on the other. If the corner is square, the distance between these two points will be exactly 5 feet. If it's more or less, determine the extent of the error on the "short" wall; that is, the one where a cabinet run terminates or has the shorter of the two runs to that corner. Adjusting the cabinets on the shorter length will require less work.

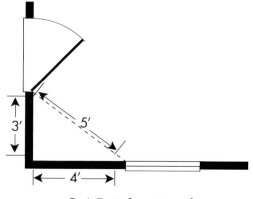

3-4-5 right triangle

7. Measure and note the exact locations and dimensions of radiators, registers, switches, receptacles, light fixtures, and, if possible, places where plumbing and gas connections come through the wall or floor.

8. When you finish a wall, add up the individual measurements and check the total against your original measurement of the entire wall. If there's any difference, start over.

9. Measure all the other walls in the same manner to complete your sketch of the room with all necessary measurements and details.

10. Measure each wall and draw detailed elevation views (including doorways, windows, and permanent fixtures), like the one *below*. When complete, your sketch should resemble the floor plan on page 96.

Include diagrams of rooms adjacent to the kitchen as well. Should your old arrangement prove confining, you may consider expanding the kitchen into these other rooms.

Make certain something won't get in the way and alter your measurements. Check all the areas affected by the remodeling for structural prob-

lems or hidden elements (big drain pipes, a furnace chimney) that could change your plans. If you need help, get advice from a building engineer, inspector, or architect.

Now you're ready to work with the layout and make rough sketches of optional floor plans (see pages 97–98), arrange templates of components on your sketches (see pages 99–101), and make a final plan (see pages 105–107).

continued

TOOLS TO USE

A few tools will make the job of drawing your new kitchen plan easier. The last four items are sold at any artist's supply store.
- ■ A 25-foot steel tape measure
- ■ ¼-inch graph paper
- ■ A roll of tracing paper
- ■ A good-quality artist's eraser
- ■ A 12-inch architect's combination ruler and scale

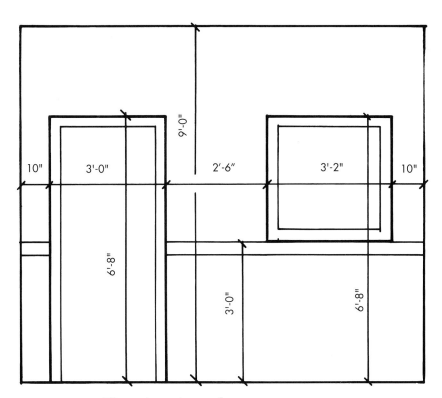

Elevation view of measurements

After you've drawn an accurate floor plan like the one shown *below,* use it as a guide for sketching your ideas. Simply lay tracing paper over the drawing and sketch in various layouts as shown on pages 97 and 98.

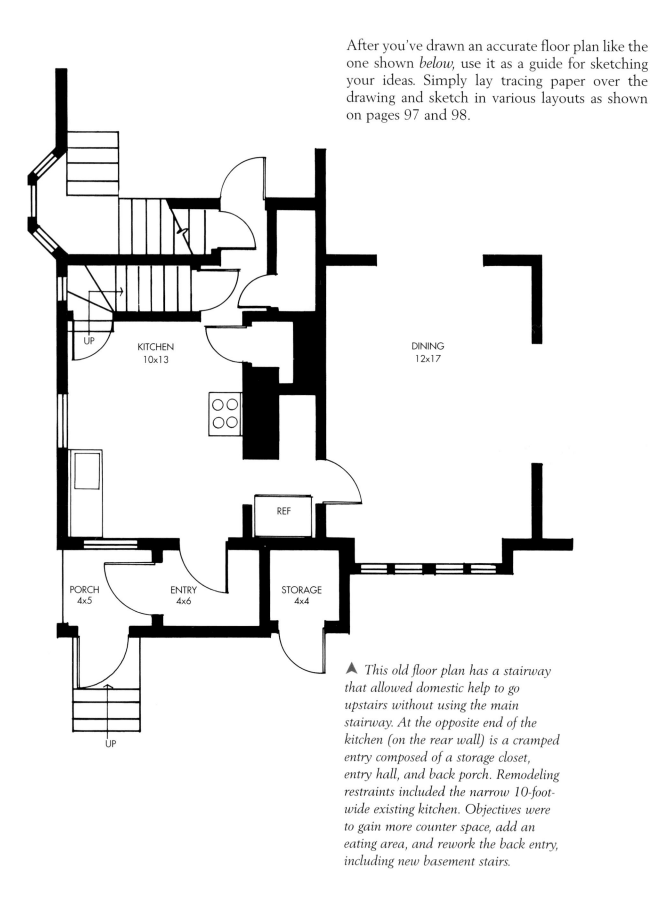

▲ *This old floor plan has a stairway that allowed domestic help to go upstairs without using the main stairway. At the opposite end of the kitchen (on the rear wall) is a cramped entry composed of a storage closet, entry hall, and back porch. Remodeling restraints included the narrow 10-foot-wide existing kitchen. Objectives were to gain more counter space, add an eating area, and rework the back entry, including new basement stairs.*

Rough Sketches

Now it's time to tinker. With the kitchen space accurately measured up on paper, make several copies of your sketch, then play a bit with a few different layouts. Maybe that U-shaped kitchen has room for an island. Maybe a peninsula could turn your L-shaped kitchen into a full or partial U. Does the range work best on the east wall or the north wall? What about the refrigerator?

Review the layout guidelines in Chapter 2 and standard dimensions on page 93, making sure you follow proper clearances. When you get close

to a final plan, fine-tune it using those guidelines.

Familiarize yourself with standard cabinet and appliance shapes and dimensions, shown as templates on pages 99–101.

Seek inspiration by reviewing your folder of design ideas.

If you're changing the location of a sink or gas appliance, make sure you stay in compliance with local building codes.

continued

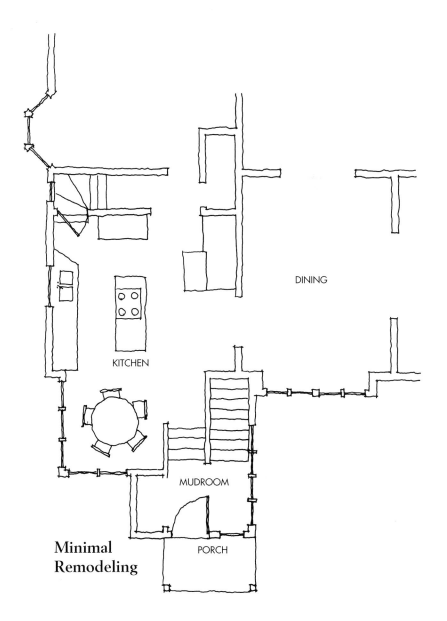

DINING

KITCHEN

MUDROOM

PORCH

Minimal Remodeling

◄ *This minimal plan leaves the stairway intact, eliminating the cost of removing it. The original rear wall is removed and a small addition built to gain a window-filled eating area, mudroom with stairs to the basement, and back porch. There's more counter space, too. One disadvantage is that traffic flow to the stairs interrupts the work space. Another is that the cooktop must be located in the narrow 2×6-foot island; in such an arrangement the ideal island should be 3 feet wide so children passing by aren't in danger of accidentally tipping over boiling pots.*

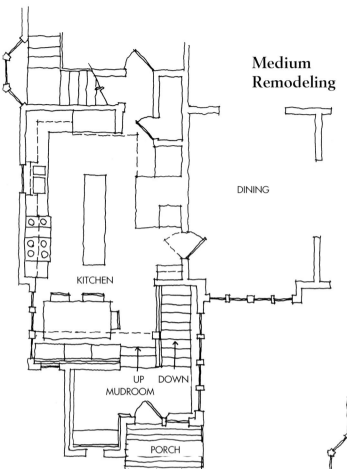

Medium Remodeling

DINING

KITCHEN

UP DOWN

MUDROOM

PORCH

◄ *In this design the kitchen stairway is removed, thus yielding a larger kitchen with more continuous counter space. By pushing out the rear of the house 11 feet and building a 140-square-foot addition, there's space for a sunny dining spot, mudroom, pantry, and new basement stairs out of the main traffic flow. The basic triangle of stove, sink, and refrigerator remains out of the traffic flow, and a 2×8-foot island adds counter space and handles recycling bins and additional storage. Bench seating built into the back wall accommodates a larger dining table in less space than in the minimal plan. An advantage of this plan is that the cooktop is located in counter space along the outside wall, not in the island.*

► *The stairway is altered in this design, becoming a part of the main stairway yet giving second-floor bedrooms a direct connection with the kitchen. This design includes 22 feet of counter space. A rear addition contains an eating area, mudroom, and back porch. New basement stairs become a central feature, creating a gentle curve around a built-in bench in the eating area. Though the cooktop is placed in the 2-foot-wide island, it could easily be adjacent to the sink.*

Given these three designs, the homeowners chose the medium design. They didn't mind the stairway's absence and of the three plans, it has lots of counter space and doesn't cost as much as the high-end design. Plumbing is moved only a few feet to relocate the sink. Gas lines are moved to the outside wall (not an expensive change) to accommodate a new high-power cooktop, which can then be vented directly outside. Old radiators were replaced with new thin-line ones. Baseboard heating is used in the mudroom.

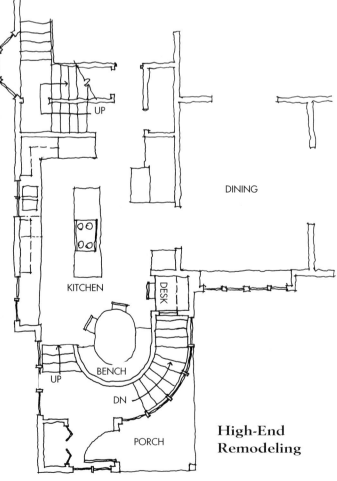

UP

DINING

KITCHEN

DESK

UP

BENCH

DN

PORCH

High-End Remodeling

Using Templates

Experiment with alternative designs using the appliance and cabinet templates here and on pages 100 and 101. Because they are drawn to a ¼-inch scale, you can arrange them on your plan until you come up with a layout you like. Place the sink and appliances first then the cabinets.

Most of these drawings show overhead (also called a plan view) and elevation views. Trace overhead views for your floor plans; draw elevations to help you visualize what a wall will look like. Although appliances or cabinets could be of various styles, the templates depict basic models—your primary concern is the space they will occupy.

To use these templates, trace or copy the cabinet and appliance shapes you need. Coloring the tracing paper with a marker makes the elements more visible on your floor plan. Cut out the outlines of cabinets and appliances (with doors open to indicate space in use) and arrange them on your rough sketches. Keep repositioning the shapes on the graph-paper floor plan until the plan suits you.

Wall Cabinets

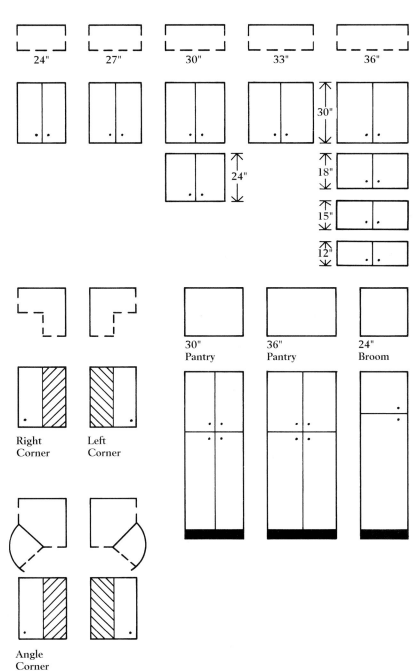

It is permissible to photocopy this page for personal, nonprofit use.

continued

Base Cabinets

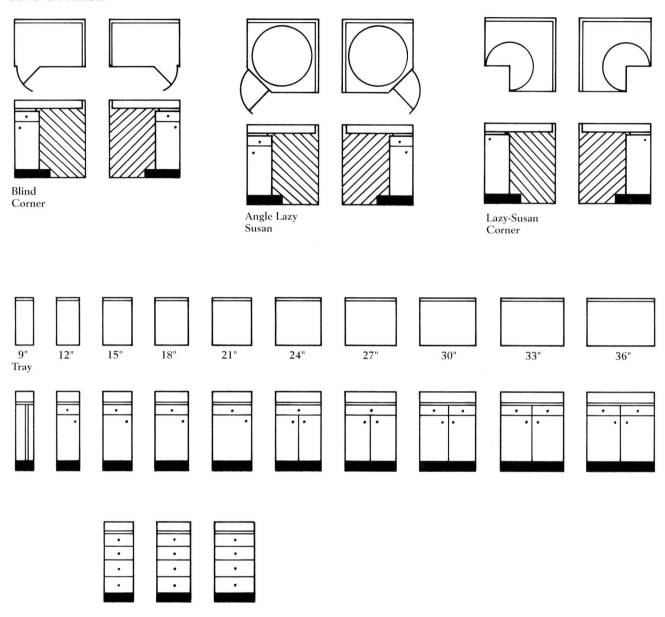

Blind
Corner

Angle Lazy
Susan

Lazy-Susan
Corner

9"
Tray

12"

15"

18"

21"

24"

27"

30"

33"

36"

Sink Bases

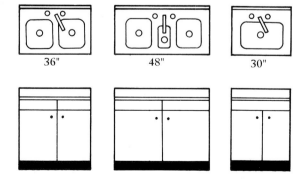

36"

48"

30"

It is permissible to photocopy this page for personal,
nonprofit use.

Appliances

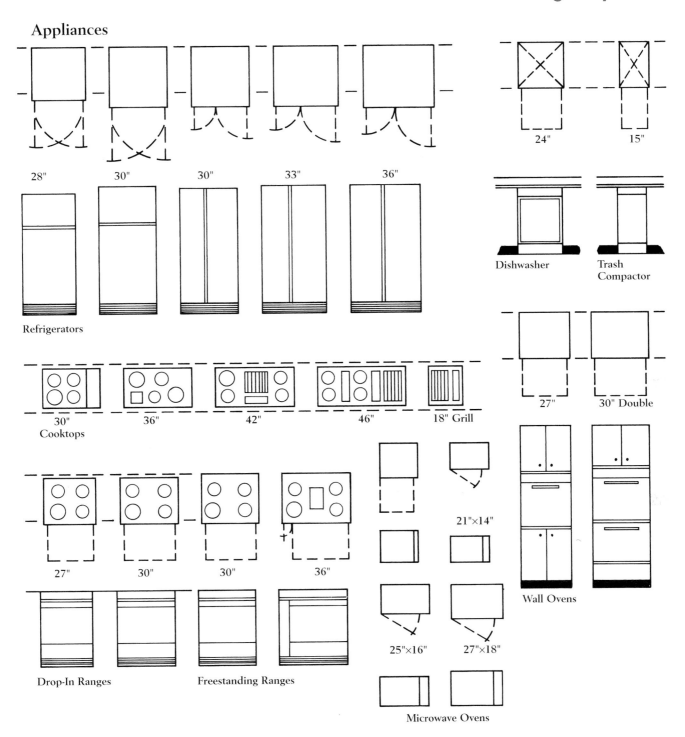

24"   15"

28"   30"   30"   33"   36"

Refrigerators

Dishwasher   Trash Compactor

30"   36"   42"   46"   18" Grill

Cooktops

27"   30" Double

27"   30"   30"   36"

21"×14"

Wall Ovens

Drop-In Ranges   **Freestanding Ranges**

25"×16"   27"×18"

Microwave Ovens

It is permissible to photocopy this page for personal, nonprofit use.

Laying Out Cabinets

For all their diversity of type and style, kitchen cabinet sizes are fairly standardized. That doesn't mean you can't buy or build to nonstandard dimensions. It's just that fixtures and appliances have been sized to coordinate with standard cabinet dimensions. These dimensions are also geared to making the most of the primary cabinet material, which is a 4×8-foot sheet of plywood.

All stock and ready-to-assemble (RTA) lines conform to these standards.

If you're buying ready-made cabinets (stock or RTA), keep in mind that base and wall units typically come in widths that vary in 3-inch increments, typically from 12 to 48 inches. To close a gap between a corner wall and the end of a cabinet run, buy a matching filler strip and cut it to the exact size of the gap.

Refrigerator Cabinets

Refrigerator cabinets are a dimensional cross between wall and base cabinets. Since they're mounted over the top of the refrigerator, they need to be reachable, so they are as deep as the refrigerator. They're also wide (approximately 36 inches) but only 18 inches high, to clear the height of a freestanding refrigerator and allow proper air circulation around it.

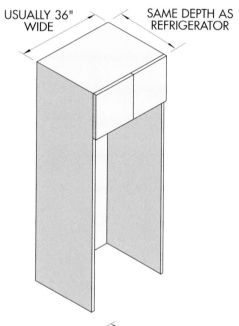

USUALLY 36" WIDE

SAME DEPTH AS REFRIGERATOR

24" DEEP

84" HIGH

Pantry Cabinets

Pantry or full-height cabinets are typically 84 inches high and 24 inches deep so they line up both with the top of the wall cabinets and the front of the base units. They often are placed next to a refrigerator or at the end of a cabinet run to store quantities of nonrefrigerated food or cooking utensils, or to serve as a broom/utility closet.

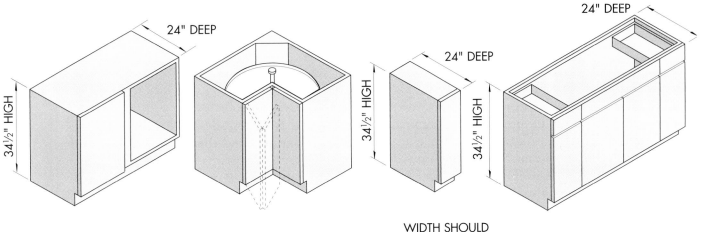

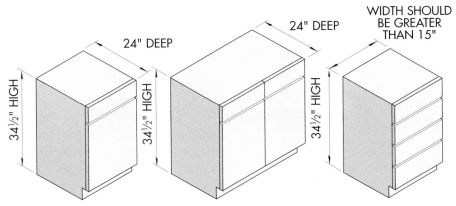

Base Cabinets

Base cabinets are 24 inches deep and 34½ inches high (to accommodate 1½-inch thick counters for a 36-inch-high work surface). Base cabinets less than 15 inches wide have limited use except for trays, so try to plan the layout with a minimum of narrow units.

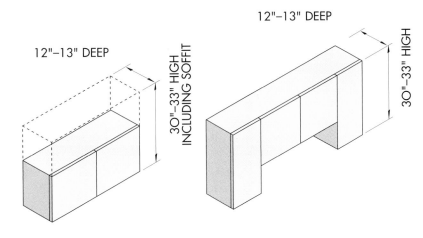

Wall Cabinets

Most wall cabinets are 12 to 13 inches deep and 30 to 33 inches high. This height allows for clearance over the counter. Wall cabinets are usually hung with the top line 84 inches from the floor. They are left open as a display shelf or topped with a flush or extended soffit going to the ceiling. For more storage, extend wall cabinets all the way to the ceiling, provided you're willing to use a step stool to reach the highest shelves.

continued

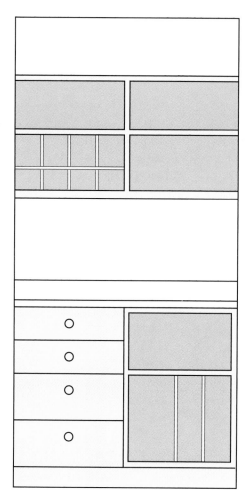

▲ *This elevation view shows the options available for storage; drawers and slots in varying sizes can fit your needs.*

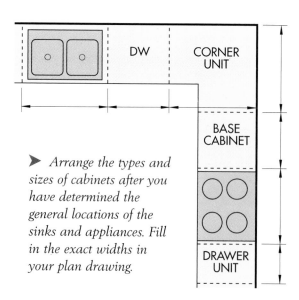

▶ *Arrange the types and sizes of cabinets after you have determined the general locations of the sinks and appliances. Fill in the exact widths in your plan drawing.*

DESIGN DETAIL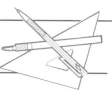

■ When considering how to group cabinets in a given amount of space, you may have more than one option. For example, 84 inches of space allows for two 42-inch cabinets or two 30-inch and one 24-inch unit. The final choice may depend on the manufacturer's specifications, if you're buying cabinets, or on what sort of door and drawer configuration you want for that particular run and for the whole kitchen.

■ Corners create a problem of inaccessible, and thus wasted, space. There are two solutions for wall and base cabinets. Diagonal cabinets are an excellent way to use this space. They can be equipped with full-circle rotating shelves for easy-access storage. If you want inside corners to be square, go with a lazy Susan cabinet with an L-shaped door. It can be fitted with pie-cut rotating shelves that fasten to the door. On a base unit, the full-height door also eliminates having drawers in the corner.

At corners of base cabinets, clearance must be provided for any projecting knobs or pulls (see diagram *below*). Corner filler panels are available for this purpose.

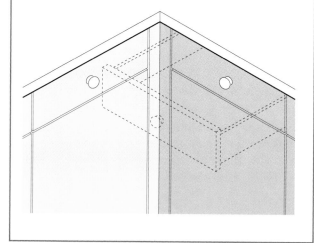

Final Plans

When you have a design that you like, you're ready to make the final plans—the working drawings. Start again on a clean sheet of graph paper and work to ½-inch scale where ½ inch equals 1 foot (see page 109). You will be working up a cabinet schedule from this plan, so think of it as a series of individual cabinets.

Use the drawing you made from measuring up the room as your starting point and again show all windows, doors, and other elements (existing gas and water lines, electrical connections, heating and/or cooling outlets). Use a ruler for straight lines and a draftsman's triangle for square corners and, if the need arises, a 45-degree angle. Keep your pencil sharp.

Along with cabinets, include specifications for the actual appliances and fixtures you'll be using.

If water or gas connections are to be moved, show it on the plan. Also show new electrical outlet, switch and fixture locations, and new heating or cooling outlets, if any. Indicate any major remodeling changes, such as new or shifted walls, doors, or windows. Shade in the new walls to differentiate them from existing walls.

Include exact dimensions of the appliances, the location and height of windows, door swings, and location of heating outlets. Also check for potential conflicts between cabinets and window or door trim. Your final drawing should contain all the elements shown on the final floor plan on page 106 of our sample kitchen.

continued

Design Tips

■ When designing a peninsula or island, consider making it 30 to 36 inches deep and having doors and drawers on both sides. The same goes for cabinets that will be hung from the ceiling and thus be open on two sides.

■ Check door swings. If a kitchen door is hinged to open against the face of an appliance, consider rehanging it on the other side of the jamb or hinging it to swing out, not in.

■ Don't install a built-in oven too high; this can result in burns and make removing pans difficult. Place it so that the open oven door is at about the same level as the counter (normally 36 inches).

■ Placement of a dishwasher in a cabinet that's perpendicular to the sink may produce a frustrating situation. When the dishwasher door is open, it may partially block access to the sink. Consider traffic flow from table to sink to dishwasher and eliminate all obstacles.

■ If at all possible, keep cooking appliances and the dishwasher (which also produces a lot of heat) away from the refrigerator. If it's not a side-by-side unit, make sure the refrigerator can be hinged so it swings away from, not into, the work area. Also make sure it swings more than 90 degrees so you can pull the shelves out for cleaning.

Final Floor Plan

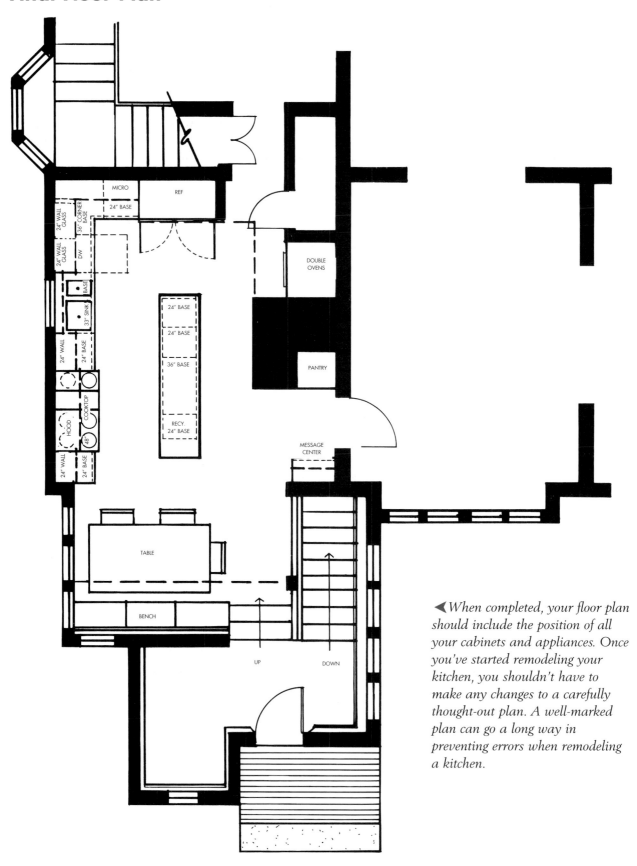

MICRO

REF

24" BASE

24" WALL GLASS

24" WALL GLASS

36" CORNER BASE

DW

BASE

33" SINK

24" WALL

24" BASE

24" WALL

HOOD

48"

COOKTOP

24" WALL

24" BASE

24" BASE

24" BASE

36" BASE

RECY.
24" BASE

DOUBLE
OVENS

PANTRY

MESSAGE
CENTER

TABLE

BENCH

UP

DOWN

◀ *When completed, your floor plan should include the position of all your cabinets and appliances. Once you've started remodeling your kitchen, you shouldn't have to make any changes to a carefully thought-out plan. A well-marked plan can go a long way in preventing errors when remodeling a kitchen.*

Elevations

An overhead floor plan view gives you a good idea how a layout occupies a space. But to see the way a kitchen is going to look to the human eye—the arrangements of doors and drawers, how wall and base cabinets relate to each other, how appliances function in a work triangle—you need elevation views. An elevation takes in one wall at a time and, like the plan view, shows the cabinets, appliances, fixtures, and outlets.

At this point, the biggest variable is with the cabinet configurations. Here are some tips for fine-tuning your cabinet faces.

■ Base cabinets up to 21 inches wide generally carry one door or a single bank of drawers. Doors shouldn't be any wider or they will swing too far out into the kitchen. Drawer cabinets can be wider, up to 24 inches.

■ Stock and RTA wall cabinets can be up to 21 inches wide in a single-door style. The main drawback comes from the wider door swinging out so far. They can be ungainly and even pose a minor hazard if left open and someone stands up under them. Keep wall cabinets to 18 inches or less.

■ Drawer cabinets often look best at the open end of a run, instead of in the middle. Try to keep them out of inside corners to avoid creating hard-to-reach storage.

■ For an orderly appearance, keep doors and drawers in vertical and horizontal alignment.

continued

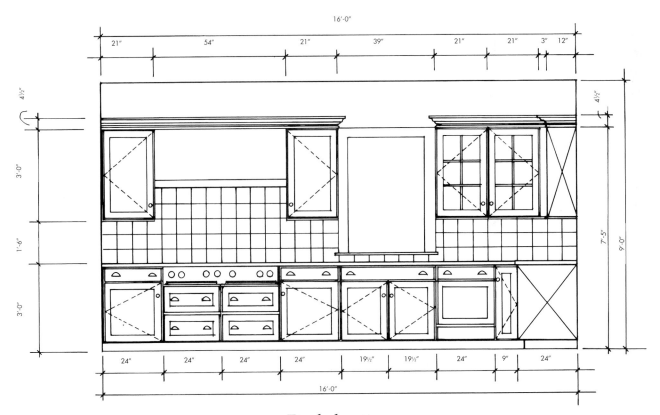

Final elevation

Final Design Checklist

■ Is there plenty of counter space between appliances?

■ Is there enough space at the corners for drawers to open fully?

■ Have you planned adjustable and roll-out shelving for the cabinets?

■ Do the cabinets come with knobs, or do they have to be selected?

■ Where will the knobs or pulls be placed on the cabinets? Will they interfere with appliance door openings?

■ Is the microwave at the right height for pulling out hot items? Can children access it?

■ Are the other appliances installed at the right height for easy access?

■ Have you planned enough under-cabinet lighting?

■ Are light fixtures planned for above the sink, cooktop, or range?

■ Has the toe kick below the cabinets been designed for the thickness of your flooring?

■ Will the new kitchen floor match the style and height of flooring in adjoining rooms?

■ Will new walls be trimmed with baseboard, or will the floor be coved?

■ How will this baseboard or cove meet the molding around the doors?

■ How will the walls be finished? Will they have to be prepared for painting or wallpaper?

■ How will the ceiling be finished?

Double-check your plan

■ **Is the work flow uninterrupted?** Traffic should flow around the kitchen's work triangle. If it doesn't, collisions are likely between the cook and anyone passing through.

■ **Is there optimum space between work centers?** It's best to allow 4 to 9 feet between the range and refrigerator, 4 to 7 feet between the refrigerator and the sink, and 4 to 6 feet between the sink and the range. Tighten up this work triangle and you've created a traffic jam. Allow too much space and you'll need track shoes to work in your kitchen.

■ **Is there counter space near each work center?** Counter space on both sides of the sink (18 to 24 inches on each side) is a given. You also need space near the refrigerator (15 inches on the handle side) to set foods, a heat-resistant space near the microwave oven and wall ovens (15 to 18 inches on one side) to set hot pans, and room around the cooktop (12 to 18 inches on each side) for supplies.

■ **Do you have enough storage space where you need it?** Basic storage standards suggest 18 square feet of cabinet space plus 6 additional square feet for each family member. Plan storage space near where the item will be used first: pot storage near the range and food storage near the mixing center, for examples. You'll need space for cool storage: 12 cubic feet (refrigerator/freezer) for two people. Add 2 cubic feet for each additional person.

■ **Can you make room for eating?** If you are short on space, consider a counter eating area that can double as food-preparation space. For a table and chairs, plan a minimum of 32 inches between the table and the wall.

Check standard dimensions

Keep in mind these standard dimensions:

■ Factory-built base cabinets are made in 3-inch increments from 12 to 48 inches wide and are 24 inches deep (front to back).

■ Wall cabinets range from 12 to 48 inches wide and 12 to 13 inches deep.

■ Appliances placed opposite one another require 5 to 6 feet of clearance so that doors can open at the same time without interference. Consider allowing at least 15 inches on either side of the range for setting hot items.

■ Counter surfaces are usually 36 inches high. Allow 15 to 18 inches clearance between a countertop and the underside of the wall cabinet above it for small appliances such as a blender, mixer, or coffeemaker.

■ For standard-depth cabinets over a sink, allow at least 30 inches above the sink rim.

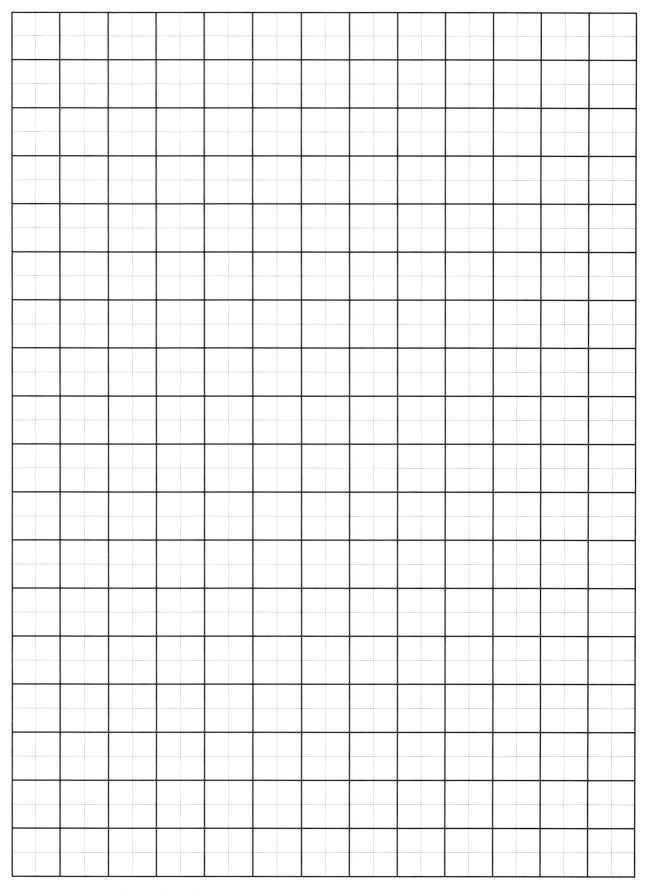

Light squares = 1 foot at ¼-inch scale
Bold squares = 1 foot at ½-inch scale

Description	Specification	Qty.	Unit	Cost	Tax	Total Cost	Cost Type	Vendor
Cabinets								
Wall cabinets 12" deep								
Base cabinets 24" deep								
Blocking—2"×4" for wall cabinets								
Island cabinet								
Pantry cabinet								
Corner lazy Susan								
Valance boards								
Mounting screws								
Cornice trim								
Floor								
Plywood underlayment—4'×8'×½"								
Flooring								
Floor felt—500-pound								
Flooring adhesive								
Flooring nails								
Quarter-round trim								
Finishing nails								
Tile								
Floor tile								
Grout compound								
Grout sealant								
Counter tile								
Tile adhesive								
Countertop								
Plywood subbase—4'×8'×¾"								
Plastic laminate								
Laminate contact adhesive								
Wood counter trim								
Butcher block								
Lights and electrical								
Track lights								
Can lights								
Ceiling light								
Sink light								
Ground fault interrupters								
Under-cabinet fixtures								

Materials and Labor Estimate

Description	Specification	Qty.	Unit	Cost	Tax	Total Cost	Cost Type	Vendor
Fixtures								
Range/oven—built-in								
Range hood								
Cooktop								
Microwave								
Trash compactor								
Refrigerator								
Garbage disposer								
Dishwasher								
Plumbing								
Kitchen sink								
Second sink								
Faucet set								
Faucet set #2								
Rough-in drain pipe								
Drain elbows								
Drain Ts								
Drain caps								
Rough-in water supply								
Water-supply elbows								
Water-supply Ts								
Water-supply caps								
Icemaker fittings								
PVC cement								
Flux solder								
Finish								
Primer paint—wall								
Primer paint—trim								
Primer paint—base coat								
Windows								
Sink								
Dining								
Labor								
Kitchen design								
Cabinet fabrication								
Cabinet installation								
Electrical								
Plumbing								
Flooring								
Carpentry—miscellaneous								
Removal of old kitchen								

Adapted with permission from *The Complete Guide to Being Your Own Remodeling Contractor* by Kent Lester (Betterway Books, Cincinnati, Ohio; 1994).

Index

Numbers in bold indicate pages with photographs.

U.S. Units to Metric Equivalents		
To convert from	Multiply by	To get
Inches	25.4	Millimeters (mm)
Inches	2.54	Centimeters (cm)
Feet	30.48	Centimeters (cm)
Feet	0.3048	Meters (m)

Metric Units to U.S. Equivalents		
To convert from	Multiply by	To get
Millimeters	0.0394	Inches
Centimeters	0.3937	Inches
Centimeters	0.0328	Feet
Meters	3.2808	Feet